EMMA DREAMWEAVER

HOW TO MAKE FRIENDS AND INFLUENCE PEOPLE

PROTAJ

CONTENTS

HOW TO MAKE FRIENDS AND INFLUENCE PEOPLE

INTRODUCTION: WHY WINNING FRIENDS AND INFLUENCING

Overview of Social Skills in Today's World

The Growing Importance of Interpersonal Skills in Both Personal and Professional Environments

In an increasingly interconnected world, where people are more connected than ever before, the value of strong interpersonal skills has never been more crucial. These skills, often referred to as "soft skills," are at the core of our personal and professional interactions. They include the ability to communicate effectively, empathize with others, and build relationships. While hard skills—such as technical proficiency or specialized knowledge—are essential in specific careers, it is interpersonal skills that often determine the long-term success of individuals in both their careers and personal lives.

The demand for interpersonal skills has grown because of the shift toward more collaborative, dynamic workplaces and social settings. As businesses globalize, teams are no longer restricted to one geographical location, which requires individuals to adapt to diverse cultural backgrounds and communicate across various platforms. This global interconnectivity means that empathy, cultural sensitivity, and emotional intelligence are essential for success, whether you're leading a multinational team, networking, or managing relationships with clients and colleagues.

In personal environments, interpersonal skills play a significant role in building strong, meaningful connections. These relationships enrich our lives, provide support, and create a sense of belonging. As more people seek meaningful personal connections amid the noise of social media and technology, interpersonal skills stand as a bridge to deeper, more satisfying relationships.

Interpersonal Skills in the Professional World

Professionally, interpersonal skills are critical in nearly every industry. From healthcare to technology, education to business, individuals who possess strong communication and relationship-building abilities often rise through the ranks more quickly than those who focus solely on technical competence. Leadership roles, for example, demand not only an understanding of the tasks at hand but also an ability to motivate, inspire, and connect with others on a human level.

Soft skills such as active listening, empathy, negotiation, conflict resolution, and team collaboration are now integral components of what many companies seek in employees. According to surveys, employers consistently rank interpersonal skills among the most important qualities in new hires. They want individuals who can navigate complex relationships, manage diverse teams, and communicate effectively with clients and customers. The ability to connect with others is crucial for organizational success and innovation, as it helps foster creativity, problem-solving, and a positive work environment.

Moreover, interpersonal skills are essential for navigating the intricacies of workplace politics and team dynamics. As individuals work within increasingly cross-functional teams, the ability to collaborate effectively with people of varying backgrounds, temperaments, and work styles is paramount. Professionals who can build rapport, mediate disputes, and inspire trust often find themselves in leadership positions, as they have the capability to unite teams and guide them toward common goals.

Interpersonal Skills in Personal Life

Outside of the professional sphere, interpersonal skills are just as vital in fostering strong relationships with family, friends, and acquaintances. Emotional intelligence—the ability to recognize and manage your emotions while also understanding and influencing the emotions of others—is essential in personal interactions. Those who excel at understanding non-verbal cues, demonstrating empathy, and providing emotional support are better equipped to maintain long-lasting and healthy relationships.

In personal contexts, these skills enable individuals to navigate difficult conversations, resolve conflicts, and cultivate deeper connections. Whether it's helping a friend through a tough time, managing a family disagreement, or simply maintaining long-term friendships, interpersonal skills like empathy, active listening, and clear communication help to create an emotional connection that stands the test of time.

While these skills have always been important, they have gained even more prominence in today's fast-paced world, where the ability to genuinely connect with others provides a much-needed respite from superficial or transactional interactions. In many ways, interpersonal skills are the foundation of emotional well-being, offering people the tools they need to build supportive networks that enrich their lives.

How Technology Has Impacted the Way We Build and Maintain Relationships

As technology continues to evolve at a rapid pace, it has undoubtedly revolutionized the way we communicate. Social media, instant messaging, and video calls have made it easier than ever to stay connected with friends, family, and colleagues from across the globe. However, while technology has facilitated communication, it has also changed the nature of our relationships, presenting both opportunities and challenges in how we develop and maintain them.

One of the most significant impacts of technology is the rise of superficial connections. While platforms like Facebook, Instagram, LinkedIn, and Twitter allow us to stay in touch with a larger network of people, these interactions are often shallow, characterized by quick exchanges or fleeting updates. While we may feel connected to a large group, the depth and quality of these relationships can suffer. Genuine emotional intimacy requires more than a "like" on a post or a brief message; it requires time, effort, and meaningful interaction.

This shift towards digital communication has created a paradox: we are more connected than ever, yet many people report feeling isolated or disconnected. A study by the American Psychological Association (APA) found that despite the prevalence of social media, feelings of loneliness have increased, especially among young adults. This suggests that while digital platforms can facilitate connection, they are not a substitute for face-to-face, emotionally rich interactions that foster genuine closeness.

The Decline of Face-to-Face Interactions

As more people rely on texting, emails, and social media to communicate, face-to-face interactions have diminished. Video conferencing tools like Zoom or Microsoft Teams have replaced many in-person meetings, particularly in professional settings. While these tools offer convenience, they also remove key elements of communication that are critical to building strong relationships—such as body language, facial expressions, and the nuances of tone.

Face-to-face communication allows for the full spectrum of emotional and non-verbal cues that help us understand one another on a deeper level. These cues include everything from eye contact and posture to micro-expressions and gestures, all of which provide important context to the words we say. When these elements are absent or reduced, as they often are in digital communication, misunderstandings can occur more easily, and it becomes harder to form genuine, lasting connections.

Additionally, face-to-face interactions foster trust and camaraderie in ways that digital communication cannot replicate. There is an inherent level of vulnerability when we interact in person, which is critical for deepening relationships. Whether it's a handshake, a shared smile, or even sitting in comfortable silence, these small moments of human interaction build rapport and emotional bonds that are difficult to achieve through screens.

For these reasons, it's essential to prioritize face-to-face interactions wherever possible. Whether it's meeting up with a friend for coffee, scheduling in-person work meetings, or attending social gatherings, maintaining regular, real-life interactions is key to fostering strong and meaningful relationships.

The Impact of Social Media on Social Skills

Another aspect of technology that has influenced our social skills is social media. While it provides a platform for people to connect, share, and engage with others, it also has the potential to diminish essential interpersonal skills. One of the primary ways it does this is by encouraging the pursuit of external validation rather than genuine connection. Many social media users have become focused on gaining likes, shares, and followers, often at the expense of authentic interaction.

This emphasis on external validation can lead to superficial interactions, where the goal is to project a certain image or persona rather than engage in meaningful conversations. As a result, many people may feel disconnected from their true selves, presenting a polished version of their lives online while struggling with deeper issues offline. This dynamic can inhibit the development of true empathy and emotional intelligence, as individuals become more concerned with managing their online presence than cultivating real relationships.

Moreover, social media can exacerbate feelings of comparison and inadequacy. When people constantly see idealized versions of others' lives, it can lead to feelings of self-doubt, jealousy, and anxiety. This, in turn, can affect their interpersonal relationships, as they may struggle with feelings of insecurity or become more guarded in their interactions.

However, social media isn't all negative. When used thoughtfully, it can enhance social skills by allowing people to practice empathy, stay connected with loved ones, and even build communities around shared interests. The key is to use these platforms in moderation and supplement them with real-life interactions that foster emotional intimacy and trust.

The Role of Emotional Intelligence in Fostering Meaningful Connections

As technology changes how we interact with one another, the role of emotional intelligence (EQ) in building and maintaining relationships has become increasingly important. Emotional intelligence refers to the ability to recognize, understand, and manage one's emotions and the emotions of others. Individuals with high emotional intelligence are better equipped to navigate social interactions, manage conflicts, and build lasting connections.

In today's world, where digital communication often lacks the emotional cues present in face-to-face interactions, emotional intelligence is essential for interpreting subtle signals, responding empathetically, and fostering deeper relationships. Emotional intelligence allows individuals to connect with others on a more meaningful level by understanding their needs, motivations, and emotions.

The Four Components of Emotional Intelligence

There are four key components of emotional intelligence, all of which play a crucial role in fostering meaningful connections:

1. **Self-awareness**: The ability to recognize and understand your emotions and how they affect your behavior and interactions with others. People with high self-awareness are better able to manage their emotions and maintain control in social situations.
2. **Self-regulation**: The ability to manage and control your emotions, especially in stressful or challenging situations.

Self-regulation helps prevent emotional outbursts or reactive behavior, enabling more thoughtful and constructive interactions.

3. **Social awareness**: This includes empathy—the ability to understand and share the feelings of others—as well as the ability to read social cues and navigate social dynamics. People with strong social awareness are skilled at recognizing and responding to the emotions of others, which helps them build rapport and trust.

4. **Relationship management**: The ability to build and maintain healthy, meaningful relationships through effective communication, conflict resolution, and collaboration. Individuals who excel in relationship management are often skilled at building networks, fostering teamwork, and resolving disputes.

Why Emotional Intelligence Matters in a Digital World

In an age where digital communication is ubiquitous, emotional intelligence has become even more important. Without the benefit of non-verbal cues like body language and facial expressions, individuals must rely on their emotional intelligence to interpret the emotions and intentions behind messages. This requires a deeper understanding of tone, context, and emotional nuance, which can be easily lost in text-based communication.

Moreover, emotional intelligence helps individuals navigate the challenges of modern relationships, where the lines between personal and professional interactions can blur. For example, responding to a tense email from a colleague requires emotional intelligence to understand the underlying emotions and craft a thoughtful response that de-escalates the situation. Similarly, maintaining friendships in a world where in-person interactions are less frequent requires emotional intelligence to ensure that relationships remain strong and supportive.

In summary, the importance of social skills in today's world cannot be overstated. As technology continues to change the way we interact, the need for strong interpersonal skills, emotional intelligence, and face-to-face connections becomes even more critical. By developing and honing these skills, individuals can build meaningful, lasting relationships that enrich both their personal and professional lives.

The Power of Personal Influence

In a world where success is increasingly determined by who you know as much as what you know, the power of personal influence cannot be overstated. Whether you're navigating the complexities of a professional career, building and maintaining relationships, or expanding your social circle, personal influence plays a vital role. Far from manipulation or control, true influence is about building mutual respect, trust, and lasting connections. This section explores how personal influence can shape your career trajectory, relationships, and social life, introduces the concept of social capital, and emphasizes why genuine influence is about fostering relationships rather than manipulation.

How Personal Influence Shapes Your Career Trajectory

Personal influence is one of the most powerful tools you can use to steer your career in the direction you desire. Whether you're looking to advance within your current organization, shift to a new industry, or start a venture of your own, the way you influence others—colleagues, superiors, clients, and even competitors—can significantly impact your success.

1. Influence in the Workplace

At work, influence is often mistaken for authority, but they're not the same. Authority is typically tied to your job title or position within an organization, while influence is something you cultivate through your actions, communication, and relationships. Even if you're not in a formal leadership position, developing your influence can help you lead teams, spearhead initiatives, and drive change.

For example, consider someone in a mid-level role who demonstrates consistent initiative, listens to others, and builds strong relationships with colleagues across departments. Over time, this person gains influence because they're perceived as dependable, innovative, and supportive. Eventually, when leadership opportunities arise, they're more likely to be promoted, not because of their title but because of the influence they've cultivated.

2. Building Credibility and Trust

In any workplace, your ability to influence others is deeply tied to the level of trust you've built. Colleagues and superiors are more likely to follow your lead or support your initiatives if they trust you. Trust is built through actions, including following through on promises, demonstrating competence, and showing a commitment to the well-being of your team.

It's also important to recognize that influence grows as you become more credible. When people see that you consistently deliver results and demonstrate expertise in your field, your influence naturally expands. You don't need to force your ideas on others because they seek you out for your input, advice, and guidance.

3. Navigating Office Politics

Influence can also help you navigate office politics without becoming entangled in them. By positioning yourself as someone who brings people together, who understands different perspectives, and who works for the good of the team, you can rise above petty disagreements and power plays.

People with high levels of personal influence understand that politics are a natural part of any organization. However, instead of engaging in harmful tactics, they focus on building alliances and advocating for mutual interests. This approach not only protects your reputation but also ensures that you maintain long-term career growth.

4. Advocating for Yourself

Personal influence is also essential when it comes to advocating for your own career advancement. Whether negotiating a raise, asking for a promotion, or seeking a new opportunity, your ability to influence others can make all the difference. The relationships you've built, the trust you've cultivated, and the value you've delivered in your role all contribute to your ability to influence key decision-makers.

Those with strong personal influence don't wait passively for others to notice their achievements. They strategically manage their careers, ensuring their contributions are visible to the right people. By doing so, they align their career trajectory with their ambitions, ultimately shaping their professional success.

How Personal Influence Shapes Relationships

Influence extends far beyond the workplace. In your personal life, the relationships you build and maintain are often shaped by how well you can connect with others, make them feel valued, and inspire mutual respect. While influence in professional contexts might focus on leadership and career growth, in personal relationships, it centers on trust, empathy, and connection.

1. The Foundation of Strong Relationships

At its core, influence in relationships is about the quality of the connection you have with others. Whether it's friendships, family dynamics, or romantic partnerships, the way you interact with others and the effort you put into understanding their needs and desires greatly influences the health and longevity of the relationship.

The most influential people in our personal lives are often those who make us feel heard, respected, and understood. They don't just assert their own opinions or desires; they're genuinely interested in what we have to say and how we feel. These are the people we turn to for advice, support, or even just companionship. They influence us not because they tell us what to do, but because they make us feel safe, valued, and connected.

2. Influence Through Empathy

One of the most powerful ways to build influence in personal relationships is through empathy. Empathy allows you to step into someone else's shoes and see the world from their perspective. By showing that you understand and care about what another person is going through, you strengthen the bond between you.

This kind of influence is not about persuasion or getting others to do what you want. Instead, it's about creating a space where both parties feel valued and understood. When people know that you care about their feelings and experiences, they're more likely to trust you, open up to you, and seek your input when making decisions.

3. Influence in Conflict Resolution

Even in personal relationships, conflicts are inevitable. How you handle these moments can either strengthen or weaken your influence. Those who can navigate disagreements with grace, patience, and empathy often find that their influence grows in the aftermath of conflict. This is because people respect and trust individuals who can remain composed, seek resolution, and avoid unnecessary drama.

When people see that you can de-escalate tense situations, approach conflicts with an open mind, and seek mutually beneficial solutions, they're more likely to turn to you for guidance in future disagreements. This level of influence is invaluable in family dynamics, friendships, and even romantic relationships, where misunderstandings can easily arise.

4. Setting Healthy Boundaries

While influence is often about connection and empathy, it's equally important to know when to set boundaries. Being influential doesn't mean saying yes to everyone or sacrificing your own needs to keep others happy. In fact, strong influencers know how to set and maintain healthy boundaries, ensuring that relationships remain balanced and mutually beneficial.

When you set boundaries, you communicate your values and priorities clearly. This not only helps you maintain your mental and emotional well-being but also earns you the respect of those around you. Over time, people learn that you're not easily swayed by pressure or guilt, and this strengthens your influence because they know where you stand and what you expect from your relationships.

The Concept of Social Capital

Personal influence is deeply intertwined with the idea of **social capital**—the networks, relationships, and connections you build over time that can provide support, opportunities, and resources. Just like financial capital, social capital can be accumulated, invested, and spent, and it plays a crucial role in determining your success.

1. What is Social Capital?

Social capital refers to the value derived from the relationships you have with others. It encompasses the trust, reciprocity, information, and cooperation that flow through your social networks. Social capital isn't just about who you know; it's about the depth of those relationships and the mutual benefits that come from them.

For example, if you have a wide network of professional contacts who respect your work, you've accumulated social capital that can open doors to new job opportunities, collaborations, or mentorships. Similarly, in personal relationships, strong social capital means you have people you can rely on for emotional support, advice, and even practical assistance when needed.

2. The Value of Social Capital

The value of social capital lies in its ability to provide access to resources that might otherwise be out of reach. In a professional context, this could mean getting a referral for a job, learning about new opportunities before they're publicly available, or having someone vouch for your skills and character. In personal contexts, social capital allows you to build a support system that enhances your emotional well-being and enriches your life.

Those with high levels of social capital often find that they can navigate challenges more easily because they have a network to lean on. Whether it's seeking advice, getting a foot in the door, or finding emotional support during tough times, social capital offers a range of benefits that money or individual effort can't easily replace.

3. Building and Maintaining Social Capital

Like any form of capital, social capital must be nurtured and maintained. It's not enough to simply meet people or collect business cards—you need to invest time and energy into building genuine relationships. This means staying in touch, offering help when needed, and being a reliable and trustworthy friend or colleague.

People who are successful at building social capital often focus on reciprocity—giving as much as they receive, if not more. They offer support, advice, and resources to others without expecting immediate returns. Over time, this creates a strong network of relationships that are based on trust and mutual benefit.

Maintaining social capital also requires ongoing effort. You can't build a relationship once and expect it to sustain itself. Regular communication, meaningful interactions, and showing appreciation for the people in your network are all essential to keeping those relationships strong.

Influence Is About Building Mutual Respect and Trust, Not Manipulation

One of the most common misconceptions about influence is that it's inherently manipulative. Many people think of influence as a way to control or coerce others into doing what you want. However, genuine influence is not about manipulation—it's about building relationships based on mutual respect, trust, and shared goals.

1. The Difference Between Influence and Manipulation

Manipulation involves using deceit or underhanded tactics to get what you want, often at the expense of others. It's a short-term strategy that may yield immediate results but damages relationships in the long run. Once people realize they've been manipulated, trust is broken, and it's incredibly difficult to regain.

Influence, on the other hand, is a positive force. It involves understanding others' needs, desires, and motivations and aligning them with your own goals in a way that benefits both parties. Rather than tricking people into doing something they wouldn't normally do, influence is about helping them see how your ideas or goals can also serve their interests.

2. Building Influence Through Trust

Trust is the foundation of influence. When people trust you, they're more likely to listen to your ideas, seek your input, and follow your lead. Trust isn't something you can demand; it must be earned through consistent, honest, and respectful behavior over time.

To build trust, you need to be transparent in your intentions, reliable in your actions, and respectful in your interactions. People should know that when they deal with you, they can expect fairness, honesty, and a genuine desire to collaborate for mutual benefit.

3. The Role of Respect in Influence

Respect is another key component of influence. People are more likely to follow someone they respect, and respect is earned by treating others with dignity, showing appreciation for their contributions, and acknowledging their perspectives.

Influence isn't about pushing your agenda or belittling others. It's about recognizing the value that others bring to the table and finding ways to work together toward common goals. When people feel respected, they're more open to your ideas and more willing to collaborate with you.

4. Influence as a Collaborative Process

True influence is collaborative, not coercive. It's about finding solutions that benefit everyone involved, whether in the workplace, in friendships, or in family dynamics. When you approach influence as a process of collaboration, rather than control, you build stronger, more resilient relationships.

Collaboration involves active listening, empathy, and open communication. It means being willing to compromise and finding ways to integrate others' perspectives into your own plans. This approach not only enhances your influence but also creates a sense of shared ownership over outcomes, making everyone more invested in success.

Building Authentic, Lasting Relationships

In a world dominated by fleeting interactions and superficial connections, building authentic, lasting relationships is more valuable than ever. While casual acquaintances may serve short-term needs, deep, meaningful relationships offer profound, long-lasting benefits in both personal and professional life. Authenticity forms the foundation of these relationships, creating genuine bonds that are essential for sustained happiness and success.

The Benefits of Fostering Long-Term, Meaningful Relationships Over Surface-Level Connections

In an age where networking often seems like a numbers game, it's easy to fall into the trap of prioritizing quantity over quality in relationships. However, surface-level connections lack the depth needed to sustain meaningful interactions over time. On the other hand, long-term, deeply connected relationships are a source of emotional and psychological fulfillment that few other aspects of life can match.

One of the most significant advantages of nurturing long-term relationships is the emotional support they provide. True friends, family members, and close colleagues form a network that offers comfort and assistance during tough times. When life throws challenges your way—whether personal setbacks or professional hurdles—it's these deep relationships that serve as a vital source of strength. The trust built over time allows for open, honest communication that alleviates stress and provides a sense of security.

Moreover, fostering lasting relationships facilitates mutual growth. Close friends and colleagues challenge you to become a better version of yourself, offering feedback and encouragement that can only come from people who know you well. Unlike surface-level acquaintances, who may hesitate to confront difficult truths, people invested in long-term relationships help you navigate personal and professional growth with honest feedback, pushing you toward self-improvement.

Beyond emotional support and growth, long-term relationships also offer reliability and trust. Surface-level connections often operate on a transactional basis, where interactions are limited to mutual benefit. However, deep relationships are built on mutual trust, where both parties can rely on each other consistently, even when there's nothing to gain in the short term. This trust is essential for navigating life's complexities and challenges, providing a secure foundation for the relationship.

The benefits of these relationships extend far beyond emotional support. People who cultivate meaningful, long-lasting relationships also experience greater overall life satisfaction. The consistency and depth that come with long-term connections create a strong sense of belonging. Whether it's with a partner, close friends, or trusted colleagues, these relationships provide continuity throughout the many phases of life, contributing significantly to happiness and fulfillment.

Professionally, long-term relationships also play a crucial role in career success. Colleagues and mentors who know you well are more likely to offer meaningful collaboration, provide growth opportunities, and support your career development. These relationships are built on mutual respect, shared goals, and a history of reliable interaction. In contrast, surface-level professional connections may yield some immediate results, but they rarely lead to the depth of collaboration and support that can drive long-term success.

Authenticity as the Foundation of Lasting Friendships and Influence

While many factors contribute to building deep, lasting relationships, none are as important as authenticity. Authenticity means being true to who you are, expressing your thoughts, emotions, and values genuinely, without attempting to conform to others' expectations. It is the cornerstone of trust, the foundation upon which meaningful relationships are built.

At its core, authenticity involves vulnerability. In a world where social media often encourages the presentation of a curated, polished version of life, authenticity can feel risky. Yet, it is this very vulnerability that allows people to form real connections. When you are honest about your struggles, fears, and desires, you invite others to do the same, creating a bond that is both deeper and more resilient than those built on superficial interactions.

Being authentic also allows you to build trust, which is essential for any relationship to flourish. People can sense when someone is being disingenuous or putting on a facade, which creates distance rather than closeness. When you are authentic, others are more likely to feel safe and comfortable around you, knowing that they are interacting with the "real" you. This sense of safety is crucial for fostering long-lasting connections because it allows for open, honest communication—a key ingredient in any successful relationship.

Authenticity doesn't mean oversharing or burdening others with all your personal issues. Instead, it involves striking a balance between openness and discernment. While it's important to be honest about your feelings, needs, and desires, being authentic also means respecting boundaries—both your own and those of others. By practicing this balance, you build relationships based on mutual understanding, where both parties feel valued and respected.

Authenticity is equally important in professional relationships. Colleagues and clients are drawn to people who are genuine because it fosters trust. In a work environment where relationships are often transactional, being authentic allows you to stand out. When you build relationships based on honesty and integrity, people are more likely to invest in you, leading to stronger professional networks and opportunities for collaboration.

Additionally, authenticity makes you a better leader. People naturally gravitate toward leaders who are transparent and genuine because it creates a culture of trust and openness. When you lead with authenticity, you empower others to do the same, fostering a work environment where communication is honest, and relationships are based on mutual respect.

How Your Network and Relationships Can Create Lasting Success and Happiness in Both Personal and Professional Spheres

While it's often said that "it's not what you know, but who you know," the truth is that success in life is determined not only by the size of your network but by the quality of the relationships within it. A strong, authentic network is one of the most valuable assets a person can cultivate, providing opportunities for collaboration, growth, and support.

In personal life, close relationships contribute significantly to overall happiness. Humans are inherently social beings, and relationships give life meaning. Whether it's the joy of shared experiences, the comfort of having someone to lean on in tough times, or the pleasure of watching someone you care about grow and succeed, meaningful relationships are integral to a happy life. People with strong, supportive networks are more likely to feel fulfilled, experience less stress, and enjoy better mental and physical health.

From a professional perspective, the value of a strong network is immense. Whether you're looking for a new job, need advice on a challenging project, or want to grow your business, your network is a powerful resource. However, the key to unlocking this resource lies not in how many people you know but in how well you know them. Deep, long-lasting professional relationships open doors to opportunities that may not be available through casual connections.

Building a strong professional network is not about transactional exchanges or superficial networking events; it's about cultivating meaningful relationships where both parties benefit. In these relationships, mutual respect and shared goals create a foundation for collaboration and support. When you invest in building real connections, people are more likely to advocate for you, offer opportunities, and support your professional development.

A well-nurtured network also acts as a safety net. In times of transition or uncertainty, whether it's a career change, starting a new venture, or navigating a difficult professional situation, your network can provide the guidance, advice, and emotional support you need. Because these relationships are built on trust and authenticity, people in your network are more likely to go the extra mile to help when you need it most.

In both personal and professional life, the key to building a strong network is consistency. Relationships, like any other aspect of life, require time and effort to maintain. It's not enough to establish a connection; you must continue to nurture it. Regular communication, offering support when needed, and being genuinely interested in the other person's life are essential components of maintaining long-lasting relationships.

By fostering authentic, lasting relationships and investing in a strong network, you create a foundation for lasting success and happiness. These connections provide emotional support, opportunities for personal and professional growth, and a sense of belonging that enriches life in meaningful ways. Whether in your personal life or your career, the effort you put into building and maintaining authentic relationships is one of the most rewarding investments you can make.

THE FOUNDATION OF CONNECTION – LISTENING MORE THAN

The Power of Active Listening

Active listening is a critical component of building meaningful relationships, whether personal or professional. It goes beyond simply hearing the words someone is saying; it involves fully engaging with the speaker and understanding their message on a deeper level. This form of listening is the cornerstone of effective communication and is essential for establishing and maintaining strong, trust-based connections with others.

The Essence of Active Listening

Active listening is not a passive activity but a dynamic process that requires your full attention and engagement. It involves several key components:

- **Focus:** To truly listen, you need to be present in the moment. This means setting aside distractions, such as your phone or computer, and giving the speaker your undivided attention.

- **Understanding:** Active listening requires that you not only hear the words but also grasp the underlying meaning and emotions conveyed by the speaker.
- **Feedback:** Providing verbal and non-verbal feedback shows the speaker that you are engaged and that their message is being received and processed.

The Importance of Active Listening in Relationships

Active listening is crucial for several reasons:

- **Building Trust:** When you listen actively, you demonstrate respect and valuing the other person's perspective. This fosters trust and strengthens the relationship.
- **Resolving Conflicts:** Effective listening helps in understanding the root cause of conflicts and finding common ground. It allows for more constructive conversations and solutions.
- **Enhancing Empathy:** By truly hearing what others are saying, you gain insight into their feelings and experiences, which deepens your empathy and connection.

Techniques to Improve Your Listening Skills

Improving your listening skills involves both verbal and non-verbal techniques. Here's a breakdown of key strategies:

Non-Verbal Cues

Non-verbal communication plays a significant role in active listening. It can reinforce your engagement and encourage the speaker to share more openly. Key non-verbal cues include:

- **Body Language:** Maintain an open and receptive posture. Avoid crossing your arms or looking away, as these can signal disinterest. Instead, lean slightly forward, nod occasionally, and use facial expressions that reflect your engagement.

- **Eye Contact:** Consistent eye contact shows that you are focused on the speaker. It conveys attentiveness and respect. However, avoid staring, which can be intimidating; instead, use natural, intermittent eye contact.
- **Facial Expressions:** Your facial expressions should align with the emotions being conveyed by the speaker. Smiling, frowning, or showing concern can demonstrate that you are emotionally attuned to the conversation.

Eye Contact

Eye contact is a powerful tool in active listening. It helps to:

- **Establish Connection:** Eye contact can create a sense of intimacy and connection, making the speaker feel heard and valued.
- **Enhance Understanding:** By maintaining eye contact, you can better gauge the speaker's emotional state and intentions, which aids in deeper comprehension.
- **Reinforce Engagement:** It signals that you are engaged and interested in what the speaker is saying, which can encourage them to open up more.

Feedback Loops

Providing feedback helps to ensure that you have understood the speaker correctly and shows that you are engaged. Effective feedback involves:

- **Paraphrasing:** Restate what the speaker has said in your own words to confirm your understanding. For example,

"So what I'm hearing is that you're concerned about the project deadline."

- **Summarizing:** Offer a summary of key points to demonstrate that you have grasped the main ideas. This can also help clarify any misunderstandings early on.
- **Asking Clarifying Questions:** If something isn't clear, ask questions to gain more information. For example, "Can you explain what you meant by that?"
- **Acknowledging Emotions:** Recognize and validate the speaker's emotions. Statements like "It sounds like you're feeling frustrated" show empathy and understanding.

Understanding How Listening Builds Trust and Empathy

Active listening is instrumental in building trust and empathy, which are fundamental for strong, lasting relationships.

Building Trust Through Active Listening

Trust is built when people feel heard and understood. Active listening helps to:

- **Demonstrate Respect:** When you listen attentively, you show that you value the other person's perspective and experiences. This respect fosters a sense of safety and trust.
- **Avoid Misunderstandings:** By actively listening and seeking clarification, you reduce the likelihood of miscommunications and misunderstandings that can erode trust.
- **Show Commitment:** Consistent, active listening conveys that you are committed to the relationship and willing to invest time and effort into understanding the other person.

Developing Empathy Through Listening

Empathy involves understanding and sharing the feelings of another person. Active listening enhances empathy by:

- **Revealing Emotions:** Through active listening, you can better perceive the emotions underlying the speaker's words. This insight helps you connect with their experiences on a deeper level.
- **Creating Emotional Bonds:** When you empathize with someone's feelings and experiences, it strengthens the emotional bond between you, fostering a deeper and more meaningful connection.
- **Encouraging Openness:** As you demonstrate empathy through listening, others are more likely to open up and share their thoughts and feelings, leading to more genuine interactions.

Practical Applications of Active Listening

In practical terms, active listening can be applied in various scenarios to build stronger relationships:

- **In Personal Relationships:** Use active listening to support friends and family members, validate their feelings, and strengthen your connections.
- **In Professional Settings:** Apply active listening in meetings and interactions with colleagues, clients, and supervisors to enhance collaboration, resolve conflicts, and build rapport.
- **In Customer Service:** Use active listening to understand and address customer concerns effectively, creating a positive experience and fostering customer loyalty.

The Power of Asking Thoughtful, Open-Ended Questions

Understanding Open-Ended Questions

Open-ended questions are a vital tool for deepening your understanding of others and fostering meaningful conversations.

Unlike closed-ended questions, which can be answered with a simple "yes" or "no," open-ended questions invite a more comprehensive response. These questions encourage individuals to elaborate on their thoughts, feelings, and experiences, providing you with richer insights into their perspectives.

The Impact of Open-Ended Questions

Open-ended questions serve several important functions in conversations:

- **Encouraging Detailed Responses:** By asking questions that require more than a one-word answer, you invite the speaker to provide additional context and detail. This helps you gain a more nuanced understanding of their message.
- **Promoting Reflection:** These questions often encourage the speaker to reflect on their experiences and emotions, leading to deeper and more meaningful conversations.
- **Facilitating Engagement:** Open-ended questions show that you are genuinely interested in the speaker's perspective and are willing to invest time and effort into understanding them.

Examples of Effective Open-Ended Questions

To effectively use open-ended questions, consider the following examples:

- **Exploring Experiences:** Instead of asking, "Did you enjoy the event?" ask, "What did you enjoy most about the event?" This encourages the speaker to share more about their experience.
- **Understanding Perspectives:** Instead of asking, "Are you satisfied with the project?" ask, "How do you feel about the progress of the project?" This allows the speaker to express their thoughts and feelings in more detail.

- **Delving into Feelings:** Instead of asking, "Are you okay?" ask, "How are you feeling about what happened?" This helps to uncover deeper emotional responses and provides a fuller picture of the speaker's state of mind.

The Role of Follow-Up Questions

Follow-up questions are crucial for maintaining the flow of the conversation and demonstrating continued interest. They show that you are actively engaged and encourage the speaker to elaborate further. Effective follow-up questions:

- **Clarify and Expand:** If something isn't clear, ask a follow-up question to gain more details. For example, "Can you tell me more about that experience?" or "What led you to that conclusion?"
- **Show Empathy:** Use follow-up questions to express empathy and understanding. For example, "How did that situation make you feel?" or "What was going through your mind at that moment?"
- **Encourage Further Reflection:** Prompt the speaker to think more deeply about their response. For example, "What do you think would have happened if you had made a different choice?" or "How has this experience influenced your perspective?"

Integrating Open-Ended Questions into Conversations

To effectively integrate open-ended questions into your conversations:

- **Be Genuine:** Ask questions that reflect your genuine curiosity and interest in the speaker's experiences and perspectives. Avoid questions that seem insincere or merely rhetorical.

- **Listen Actively:** Pay close attention to the speaker's responses and use their answers to guide your follow-up questions. This demonstrates that you are engaged and responsive to their input.
- **Balance Questioning with Listening:** While open-ended questions are important, balance them with active listening. Allow the speaker to share their thoughts without interruption and be mindful of their cues and emotions.

Understanding and Connecting on a Deeper Level

Active listening is more than just a communication skill; it is an essential practice for gaining deeper insights into people's emotions, motivations, and goals. This section explores how active listening can lead to a profound understanding of others and provides techniques for interpreting what's not being said. Additionally, it highlights how effective listening helps in building rapport, respect, and influence in relationships.

How Active Listening Leads to Deeper Insights

Active listening allows you to grasp not just the content of what someone is saying, but also the emotions and motivations behind their words. Here's how active listening can lead to a deeper understanding:

- **Uncovering Emotions:** By focusing on how a person expresses themselves, including their tone of voice, facial expressions, and body language, you can gain insights into their emotional state. For instance, if someone's voice trembles or their shoulders slump while discussing a topic, it might indicate underlying sadness or stress. Recognizing these emotional cues helps you understand what they are truly feeling, beyond the words they use.
- **Identifying Motivations:** Motivations often drive behaviors and decisions. Active listening helps you uncover these

motivations by paying attention to the context and subtext of the conversation. For example, if a colleague frequently talks about their dissatisfaction with their role, it may reveal a deeper motivation related to career advancement or recognition. Understanding these motivations allows you to align your support or responses with their true needs.

· **Understanding Goals:** People's goals and aspirations shape their actions and decisions. Through active listening, you can discern these goals by noting recurring themes or desires in their conversations. For example, if a friend often mentions their dream of starting a business, it provides insight into their long-term aspirations and can guide how you offer support or advice.

Techniques for Interpreting What's Not Being Said

Effective listening involves interpreting not just the spoken words but also the unspoken messages. Here are some techniques for reading between the lines:

· **Observing Non-Verbal Cues:** Pay attention to non-verbal signals such as facial expressions, posture, and gestures. For instance, crossed arms might suggest defensiveness or discomfort, while a relaxed posture could indicate openness. These cues can provide additional context to the spoken message and reveal underlying feelings or attitudes.

· **Analyzing Emotional Subtext:** Listen for emotional undertones that may not be explicitly stated. For example, a person might express frustration in a mild tone, but the emotional intensity could be much stronger. Understanding these subtleties helps you grasp the full emotional impact of their message.

· **Recognizing Discrepancies:** Note any discrepancies between what is said and how it is said. If someone says they are fine but their tone and body language suggest otherwise, it may indicate that they are not being entirely honest about their feelings. Addressing these discrepancies can lead to more honest and open communication.

· **Asking Clarifying Questions:** When in doubt, ask questions to clarify the speaker's true intentions or feelings. For example, "Can you help me understand what you're really concerned about?" This approach encourages the speaker to elaborate and provides you with a clearer picture of their underlying thoughts and emotions.

How Listening Helps You Build Rapport, Respect, and Influence

Active listening is a powerful tool for building and maintaining strong relationships. Here's how it contributes to rapport, respect, and influence:

· **Building Rapport:** Rapport is the sense of mutual understanding and connection between individuals. Active listening fosters rapport by showing that you genuinely care about the other person's perspective. When people feel heard and understood, they are more likely to develop a positive and trusting relationship with you. For example, actively listening to a colleague's concerns about a project can help build a collaborative and supportive working relationship.

· **Earning Respect:** Respect is earned through consistent, respectful interactions. By listening actively, you demonstrate that you value the other person's opinions and experiences. This validation of their viewpoints helps to establish and maintain respect. Additionally, thoughtful responses based on what you've heard further reinforce this respect and show that you are genuinely engaged in the conversation.

- **Enhancing Influence:** Influence involves guiding and persuading others in a positive way. Active listening enhances your influence by helping you understand others' needs, preferences, and motivations. This understanding allows you to tailor your approach to align with their interests, making your interactions more impactful. For example, if you understand a colleague's career goals, you can offer advice or support that is directly relevant to their aspirations, thereby increasing your influence in their decision-making process.

Practical Applications of Active Listening

Active listening can be applied in various scenarios to enhance your relationships and interactions:

- **In Personal Relationships:** Use active listening to support and connect with friends and family members. By paying attention to their feelings and needs, you can offer meaningful support and strengthen your personal bonds.
- **In Professional Settings:** Apply active listening in meetings, one-on-one conversations, and team interactions. This practice helps you build rapport with colleagues, resolve conflicts, and foster a positive work environment.
- **In Customer Service:** Active listening is crucial for understanding and addressing customer concerns. By listening attentively to customer feedback and needs, you can provide effective solutions and build strong customer relationships.

THE ART OF EMPATHY – WALKING IN SOMEONE ELSE'S SHO

Understanding Empathy and Its Role in Building Relationships

Empathy is a fundamental component of effective communication and strong relationships. It goes beyond mere sympathy, where one might feel pity or sorrow for another's situation. Instead, empathy involves a deeper, more nuanced understanding of another person's experiences and emotions. By genuinely engaging with someone else's feelings and perspectives, you build stronger, more meaningful connections. This section explores the essence of empathy, its crucial role in relationship-building, and the two distinct yet complementary forms of empathy: cognitive and emotional.

Defining Empathy and Its Role in Creating Strong, Lasting Connections

Empathy is the ability to perceive and relate to the emotions and experiences of others. It's a bridge between individuals that fosters understanding and connection. At its core, empathy involves:

- **Perspective-Taking**: This is the ability to put yourself in someone else's shoes and see the world from their point of view. It requires an open mind and a willingness to understand experiences different from your own.
- **Emotional Resonance**: Empathy also involves feeling what others are feeling. This emotional resonance means that you can sense the emotions of others as if they were your own, which strengthens your emotional connection with them.
- **Validation**: Empathy entails validating someone's feelings and experiences. It shows that their emotions are acknowledged and respected, which is essential for building trust and rapport.

The role of empathy in building relationships cannot be overstated. It is through empathetic interactions that we forge genuine connections, demonstrate support, and cultivate mutual respect. When people feel understood and valued, they are more likely to engage openly and build a lasting bond. Empathy enables us to respond to others' emotional needs effectively, making it a cornerstone of effective interpersonal communication.

How Empathy Helps You Respond to Others' Emotional Needs and Perspectives

Empathy is pivotal in responding to others' emotional needs and perspectives. Here's how:

- **Enhancing Communication**: When you practice empathy, you become more attuned to the emotions and needs of those around you. This sensitivity improves your ability to communicate effectively, as you can tailor your responses to address the emotional context of the conversation. By acknowledging and validating their feelings, you make your communication more relevant and supportive.
- **Facilitating Support**: Understanding someone's emotional state allows you to provide more meaningful support. Whether offering comfort during a tough time or celebrating successes, empathetic responses align with the person's emotional needs. This responsiveness demonstrates that you are invested in their well-being, reinforcing the strength of your relationship.
- **Resolving Conflicts**: Empathy is crucial in conflict resolution. By comprehending both sides of an argument and the emotions involved, you can find common ground and facilitate constructive dialogue. Empathetic listening helps uncover underlying issues and fosters a collaborative approach to solving problems.
- **Fostering Trust**: When people feel that their emotions and perspectives are genuinely understood, trust is built. Empathy creates a safe space where individuals are more likely to be open and honest, knowing their feelings will be met with understanding rather than judgment.

The Difference Between Cognitive Empathy and Emotional Empathy, and Why Both Are Essential

Empathy encompasses various dimensions, including cognitive and emotional empathy. Both are essential for fully engaging with others' experiences and fostering strong relationships.

- **Cognitive Empathy**: This form of empathy involves understanding another person's thoughts, beliefs, and perspectives. It's about intellectually grasping what someone else is going through without necessarily feeling their emotions. Cognitive empathy allows you to comprehend the rationale behind someone's actions or reactions and to anticipate their needs or responses. This type of empathy is crucial for effective problem-solving and communication, as it helps you understand where others are coming from and how to address their concerns thoughtfully.
- **Emotional Empathy**: Emotional empathy, on the other hand, involves sharing and resonating with another person's feelings. It's the ability to emotionally connect with someone's experiences and to feel what they are feeling. This form of empathy is vital for forming deep emotional bonds and demonstrating compassion. It allows you to respond with genuine care and support, as you can directly relate to the emotional state of others.

While cognitive empathy helps you understand the "why" behind someone's actions or feelings, emotional empathy helps you connect with the "how" they are experiencing those emotions. Both forms are essential for creating comprehensive and supportive interactions. Cognitive empathy provides the framework for understanding others, while emotional empathy fosters the depth of connection that builds trust and rapport.

In summary, empathy is a multifaceted skill that plays a critical role in building strong, meaningful relationships. By understanding and engaging with both cognitive and emotional aspects of empathy, you can enhance your communication, support, and conflict resolution abilities, ultimately fostering deeper and more authentic connections with others.

Emotional Intelligence and Empathy

The Role of Emotional Intelligence (EQ) in Personal and Professional Success

Emotional Intelligence (EQ) is the ability to recognize, understand, manage, and utilize emotions effectively in oneself and others. Unlike traditional intelligence, which focuses on cognitive abilities, EQ emphasizes the importance of emotional skills in personal and professional settings. Its role in success is profound and multifaceted:

- **Enhanced Communication**: High EQ individuals are adept at understanding and managing their own emotions while also perceiving the emotional states of others. This dual capability facilitates clearer, more empathetic communication, reducing misunderstandings and fostering stronger relationships.
- **Better Conflict Resolution**: Emotional intelligence equips individuals with the skills to navigate and resolve conflicts effectively. By managing emotions and understanding the perspectives of others, those with high EQ can address issues constructively and find mutually beneficial solutions.
- **Increased Empathy**: A key component of EQ, empathy allows individuals to connect deeply with others. This under-

standing can improve team dynamics, enhance customer relations, and foster supportive work environments.

- **Improved Leadership**: Leaders with high emotional intelligence can inspire and motivate their teams by recognizing and addressing the emotional needs of their employees. They lead with empathy, creating an environment where team members feel valued and understood.
- **Personal Growth**: EQ contributes to personal well-being by helping individuals manage stress, navigate social complexities, and build fulfilling relationships. By understanding and regulating their own emotions, individuals can achieve greater personal satisfaction and resilience.

In both personal and professional contexts, emotional intelligence plays a critical role in achieving success. It enables individuals to interact more effectively, manage relationships better, and handle challenges with greater ease.

How to Develop Emotional Intelligence Through Self-Awareness, Self-Regulation, Motivation, Empathy, and Social Skills

Developing emotional intelligence involves honing several key competencies:

- **Self-Awareness**: Self-awareness is the foundation of emotional intelligence. It involves recognizing and understanding your own emotions, strengths, and weaknesses. To enhance self-awareness:
  - **Reflect Regularly**: Take time to reflect on your emotional responses and behavior. Journaling or meditation can help you become more attuned to your emotional state.

- ○ **Seek Feedback**: Constructive feedback from others can provide valuable insights into your emotional tendencies and areas for growth.
- **Self-Regulation**: Self-regulation involves managing your emotions in a constructive manner. This competency helps in maintaining composure and responding thoughtfully rather than reacting impulsively. To improve self-regulation:
  - ○ **Practice Mindfulness**: Techniques such as deep breathing, meditation, and mindfulness exercises can help you stay calm and focused.
  - ○ **Develop Coping Strategies**: Identify and implement strategies for managing stress and emotions, such as physical exercise, hobbies, or talking with a trusted friend.
- **Motivation**: Motivation is about harnessing emotions to stay focused and achieve goals. It involves setting and pursuing goals with enthusiasm and resilience. To cultivate motivation:
  - ○ **Set Clear Goals**: Define specific, achievable goals and break them down into manageable steps.
  - ○ **Celebrate Achievements**: Recognize and celebrate your progress and accomplishments to maintain motivation and reinforce positive behavior.
- **Empathy**: Empathy involves understanding and sharing the feelings of others. To enhance empathy:
  - ○ **Listen Actively**: Practice active listening by giving full attention, reflecting on what is said, and responding with understanding.
  - ○ **Put Yourself in Others' Shoes**: Try to see situations from others' perspectives and acknowledge their emotions and experiences.

- **Social Skills**: Social skills encompass the ability to interact effectively with others. This includes building and maintaining relationships, managing conflicts, and communicating clearly. To develop social skills:
  - **Improve Communication**: Focus on clear, respectful, and effective communication, including non-verbal cues.
  - **Build Relationships**: Invest time in building and nurturing relationships through trust, support, and collaboration.

By actively working on these components, individuals can enhance their emotional intelligence, leading to improved interactions, better conflict resolution, and more effective leadership.

Real-Life Examples of How Empathy Drives Leadership and Collaboration

Empathy is a driving force behind effective leadership and collaboration. Here are some real-life examples illustrating how empathy can significantly impact these areas:

- **Leadership**: Satya Nadella, CEO of Microsoft, is often cited as an example of a leader with high emotional intelligence. His empathetic leadership style has transformed Microsoft's corporate culture. Nadella emphasizes understanding and valuing employees' perspectives, which has fostered a more inclusive and innovative work environment. His approach has led to increased employee engagement, collaboration, and overall company performance.
- **Collaboration**: In the healthcare sector, empathy plays a crucial role in patient care and team dynamics. For instance, Dr. Paul Farmer, co-founder of Partners In Health,

has demonstrated how empathy can drive collaboration in addressing global health challenges. His work emphasizes understanding the experiences of underserved populations and working collaboratively with local communities to develop effective health interventions. This empathetic approach has improved patient outcomes and strengthened partnerships across various organizations.

· **Customer Service**: Companies like Zappos have built their reputations on empathetic customer service. Zappos employees are trained to engage with customers genuinely and address their needs with empathy and understanding. This approach has resulted in high customer satisfaction, loyalty, and a strong brand reputation.

· **Team Dynamics**: In collaborative work environments, empathy can enhance team dynamics and productivity. For example, Google's Project Aristotle study highlighted that psychological safety, which is closely linked to empathy, is a key factor in high-performing teams. Teams that practice empathy and create a safe space for open communication tend to be more effective and innovative.

These examples illustrate that empathy is not just a personal attribute but a strategic advantage in leadership and collaboration. By fostering understanding and connection, empathy enhances team performance, drives organizational success, and improves overall outcomes.

Strategies for Making Others Feel Valued

Ways to Express Empathy in Everyday Interactions

Expressing empathy is key to making others feel valued and understood. Here are some effective strategies for incorporating empathy into everyday interactions:

1. **Validating Feelings**: Validation involves acknowledging and affirming someone's emotions without judgment. It shows that you recognize and respect their feelings, even if you may not fully understand or agree with them.
   - **How to Validate**: Use phrases like "I can see why you'd feel that way" or "That sounds really tough." This lets the person know that their emotions are legitimate and that their perspective is important to you.
2. **Mirroring Emotions**: Mirroring involves reflecting the emotional state of the person you're interacting with. This technique helps to demonstrate that you are in tune with their feelings and can foster a deeper connection.
   - **How to Mirror**: Pay attention to the person's tone of voice, facial expressions, and body language. If they seem excited, match their enthusiasm in your response. If they're distressed, convey empathy through a concerned tone or supportive words.
3. **Offering Emotional Support**: Emotional support involves providing comfort and reassurance to someone who is experiencing difficulty. It shows that you care about their well-being and are willing to be there for them.
   - **How to Offer Support**: Express your willingness to listen and be present. For example, "I'm here if you want to talk" or "Let me know how I can help" demon-

strates your commitment to supporting them through their challenges.

Building Trust by Showing Genuine Concern for Others' Well-Being

Building trust is a fundamental aspect of any strong relationship, and showing genuine concern for others' well-being is essential in this process. Here's how you can build trust through empathetic actions:

1. **Consistent Check-Ins**: Regularly ask about the well-being of those around you, whether they are colleagues, friends, or family. This demonstrates that you care about their overall happiness and not just about specific issues.
   - **Example**: "How have you been since our last conversation? Is there anything you'd like to talk about?"
2. **Acting on Concerns**: When someone shares their concerns with you, take action to address them whenever possible. This shows that you are not just offering empty words but are genuinely invested in their welfare.
   - **Example**: If a colleague mentions being overwhelmed with workload, offer to help with specific tasks or advocate for them with management.
3. **Being Reliable**: Reliability fosters trust. Follow through on promises and commitments, and be there for others when they need you. This builds a reputation for dependability and reinforces your concern for their well-being.
   - **Example**: If you promise to assist with a project or provide support, ensure that you deliver on that promise in a timely manner.
4. **Providing Constructive Feedback**: Offer feedback in a way that is supportive and focuses on growth. Frame your

feedback positively and constructively to help others improve while showing that you care about their development.

- ◦ **Example**: "I noticed you've been working hard on this project. One area for improvement might be X, but your efforts have been really impressive overall."

Cultivating a Habit of Empathy in Challenging or Tense Situations

Cultivating empathy, especially in challenging or tense situations, requires intentional practice and self-awareness. Here's how to maintain empathetic behavior even when interactions are difficult:

1. **Pause and Reflect**: When faced with a tense situation, take a moment to pause before responding. This brief reflection helps you avoid knee-jerk reactions and allows you to approach the situation with a clearer, more empathetic mindset.
   - ◦ **Strategy**: Practice deep breathing or count to ten to create a space between your emotional reaction and your response.
2. **Acknowledge Emotional States**: Recognize and validate the emotions of others, even if you disagree with their perspective. This shows that you respect their feelings and are willing to engage with them empathetically.
   - ◦ **Strategy**: Use phrases like "I understand that you're upset about this" or "I can see why this is frustrating for you."
3. **Seek Common Ground**: In tense interactions, finding common ground can help bridge differences and foster a

sense of connection. Focus on shared goals or interests to reframe the conversation in a more collaborative light.

- **Strategy**: Identify mutual objectives or values and emphasize them to shift the focus from conflict to cooperation.

4. **Practice Active Listening**: Ensure that you are truly listening to the other person's perspective rather than preparing your rebuttal. Active listening involves fully engaging with their message and responding thoughtfully.

- **Strategy**: Summarize or paraphrase what the other person has said to confirm your understanding and show that you are engaged in the conversation.

5. **Manage Your Own Emotions**: Keep your own emotions in check to avoid escalating the situation. By maintaining composure, you can respond more empathetically and effectively.

- **Strategy**: Develop self-regulation techniques such as mindfulness or stress management practices to help you stay calm under pressure.

6. **Empathize with the Other's Perspective**: Put yourself in the other person's position to better understand their feelings and motivations. This empathetic perspective can guide you in responding with greater sensitivity and care.

- **Strategy**: Ask yourself how you would feel in their situation and use this understanding to inform your response.

By integrating these strategies into your interactions, you can consistently make others feel valued and understood, even in challenging situations. Cultivating empathy requires ongoing effort and self-awareness, but it ultimately leads to stronger, more meaningful connections and improved relational dynamics.

BECOMING A PEOPLE MAGNET – THE POWER OF POSITIVITY

The Role of Positivity in Influencing Others

How a Positive Attitude Influences Your Ability to Win Friends and Create Lasting Relationships

A positive attitude plays a crucial role in forming and sustaining relationships. When you approach interactions with optimism and enthusiasm, it significantly impacts how others perceive and respond to you. Here's how a positive attitude influences your ability to build lasting connections:

1. **Fostering Approachability**: People are naturally drawn to individuals who exude positivity. A warm, upbeat demeanor makes you appear more approachable and friendly, encouraging others to engage with you. This initial attraction can

pave the way for deeper connections and lasting friendships.

- ◦ **Example**: In social settings, a smile and friendly conversation can make you more inviting, leading to more meaningful interactions and relationship-building opportunities.

2. **Creating a Supportive Environment**: Positivity can transform interactions by creating a supportive and encouraging environment. When you maintain a positive outlook, you are more likely to offer constructive feedback, celebrate others' successes, and support them through challenges. This supportive approach builds trust and strengthens relationships.

- ◦ **Example**: At work, a manager who consistently provides positive reinforcement and constructive feedback can motivate their team, fostering a collaborative and trusting environment.

3. **Encouraging Open Communication**: A positive attitude facilitates open and honest communication. When people feel comfortable and valued, they are more likely to share their thoughts and feelings, leading to more meaningful and transparent interactions.

- ◦ **Example**: Friends and colleagues are more likely to confide in someone who listens attentively and responds with understanding and encouragement.

4. **Enhancing Relationship Resilience**: Relationships often face challenges and conflicts. A positive attitude can help navigate these difficulties by maintaining a focus on solutions rather than problems. This resilience can help sustain relationships through tough times.

- ◦ **Example**: In a disagreement with a friend, approaching the situation with a positive mindset can lead to constructive problem-solving and the strengthening of the bond.

The Psychological and Social Benefits of Maintaining Optimism and Enthusiasm

Maintaining optimism and enthusiasm not only benefits your relationships but also has profound psychological and social benefits. Here's how a positive outlook impacts both your well-being and interactions with others:

1. **Boosting Mental Health**: Positivity is closely linked to improved mental health. An optimistic mindset can reduce stress, anxiety, and depressive symptoms by fostering a sense of hope and resilience. This psychological well-being enhances your ability to interact positively with others.
   - **Example**: Regular practice of positive thinking techniques, such as gratitude journaling or mindfulness, can improve overall mood and mental health.
2. **Enhancing Physical Health**: Studies have shown that a positive attitude can have beneficial effects on physical health, including lower blood pressure, reduced risk of chronic diseases, and improved immune function. Better physical health can contribute to more vibrant and engaging interactions with others.
   - **Example**: Engaging in physical activities with a positive attitude can lead to better fitness and increased energy, enhancing your interactions with friends and family.
3. **Strengthening Social Connections**: Optimism and enthusiasm are key drivers of social connections. People are naturally drawn to those who exhibit positive energy and

enthusiasm, leading to more social interactions and opportunities for relationship-building.

- ◦ **Example**: At social gatherings, a person who actively engages in conversations with enthusiasm and a positive outlook is more likely to attract and maintain friendships.

4. **Increasing Resilience**: Positivity fosters resilience, enabling you to bounce back from setbacks and challenges with a constructive attitude. This resilience not only benefits your personal growth but also helps you maintain strong relationships through difficulties.

- ◦ **Example**: In the face of a career setback, maintaining a positive attitude allows you to approach the situation with a growth mindset, leading to new opportunities and continued support from your network.

Why Positivity is Contagious and Attracts People to You

Positivity has a contagious effect that can significantly influence those around you. Here's why a positive attitude tends to attract people and foster social connections:

1. **Creating a Uplifting Atmosphere**: Positive individuals often create an uplifting and enjoyable atmosphere that others are eager to be part of. This positive environment encourages people to engage and participate, reinforcing connections and relationships.

- ◦ **Example**: A colleague who consistently brings energy and optimism to team meetings can inspire others to contribute positively and collaborate more effectively.

2. **Encouraging Positive Interactions**: Positivity can lead to more positive interactions and experiences. When you approach situations with a positive attitude, it tends to elicit

positive responses from others, creating a cycle of mutual encouragement and support.

- **Example**: Complimenting and encouraging others in a social setting can prompt them to reciprocate with similar positive behavior, strengthening the relationship.

3. **Building Trust and Credibility**: A consistently positive attitude helps build trust and credibility. When people perceive you as optimistic and enthusiastic, they are more likely to trust your intentions and view you as a reliable and supportive individual.

- **Example**: In a professional setting, a leader who consistently demonstrates optimism and enthusiasm can build trust among their team, leading to increased respect and loyalty.

4. **Enhancing Group Dynamics**: Positivity can enhance group dynamics by fostering a collaborative and supportive environment. When you bring a positive attitude to group settings, it encourages others to contribute and work together more effectively.

- **Example**: During a team project, a positive team member can help maintain morale and encourage collaboration, leading to better group cohesion and success.

By embracing and cultivating a positive attitude, you can influence others in meaningful ways, enhancing your personal and professional relationships. Positivity not only benefits your own well-being but also attracts and inspires those around you, leading to more fulfilling and lasting connections.

Radiating Confidence and Positivity in Social Interactions

How to Project Confidence Without Arrogance

Projecting confidence in social interactions is key to establishing yourself as a trustworthy and engaging presence. However, it's important to strike the right balance to avoid crossing the line into arrogance. Here are some strategies for projecting confidence gracefully:

1. **Maintain Open Body Language**: Confidence is often conveyed through body language. Stand tall with your shoulders back, and make eye contact to show that you are engaged and self-assured. Avoid crossing your arms, which can appear defensive or closed off.
   - **Example**: In a networking event, maintaining an upright posture and making steady eye contact while speaking and listening demonstrates confidence and openness.
2. **Use Clear and Assertive Communication**: Speak clearly and assertively, but avoid dominating the conversation. Listen actively to others, show genuine interest, and contribute thoughtfully. This approach helps you convey confidence without overshadowing others.
   - **Example**: During a team meeting, clearly articulate your ideas and suggestions while also acknowledging and building on the contributions of others.
3. **Acknowledge Your Strengths and Weaknesses**: Confident individuals are aware of their strengths and weaknesses. Emphasize your strengths without downplaying or exaggerating them. Similarly, acknowledge areas where you

are working to improve, which demonstrates humility and self-awareness.

- ◦ **Example**: In a job interview, discuss your key skills and achievements confidently while also mentioning areas you're actively developing or seeking to improve.

4. **Practice Self-Compassion**: Confidence also comes from treating yourself with kindness and understanding. Accepting that it's okay to make mistakes and being kind to yourself helps maintain a balanced perspective and project authentic confidence.

- ◦ **Example**: If you make a mistake during a presentation, acknowledge it calmly and move on, demonstrating self-compassion and confidence in your ability to handle the situation.

Techniques for Exuding Warmth, Openness, and Enthusiasm in Social Settings

Exuding warmth, openness, and enthusiasm can greatly enhance your social interactions and make others feel valued and comfortable. Here are some techniques to achieve this:

1. **Engage in Active Listening**: Show that you are genuinely interested in the conversation by actively listening and responding to what others say. Nod in agreement, paraphrase their points, and ask open-ended questions to demonstrate your engagement.

- ◦ **Example**: When conversing with a friend, reflect back on what they've shared and ask follow-up questions to show that you are truly interested in their experience.

2. **Smile and Use Positive Facial Expressions**: A warm smile and positive facial expressions can convey friendliness and approachability. Smiling not only makes you appear more inviting but also helps to create a positive atmosphere in your interactions.

   ◦ **Example**: At a social gathering, greet people with a genuine smile and maintain positive facial expressions to create a welcoming environment.

3. **Use Enthusiastic and Encouraging Language**: Choose words and phrases that express enthusiasm and encouragement. Compliment others, offer words of support, and celebrate their achievements to create a positive and uplifting interaction.

   ◦ **Example**: During a team project, acknowledge your colleagues' contributions with enthusiastic praise and encouragement to boost morale and foster a positive team dynamic.

4. **Show Genuine Curiosity and Appreciation**: Demonstrate a sincere interest in others by asking about their experiences, interests, and opinions. Express appreciation for their perspectives and contributions, which fosters a sense of connection and mutual respect.

   ◦ **Example**: When meeting someone new, ask about their hobbies or recent experiences and listen attentively to their responses, showing genuine curiosity and appreciation.

How to Stay Positive Even in Challenging or Uncertain Situations, and Why Resilience Enhances Your Ability to Influence Others

Maintaining a positive outlook in challenging or uncertain situations is crucial for sustaining influence and fostering strong relationships. Here's how to stay positive and why resilience enhances your ability to influence others:

1. **Focus on Solutions Rather Than Problems**: In difficult situations, concentrate on finding solutions and taking proactive steps. This forward-thinking approach not only helps you navigate challenges more effectively but also demonstrates resilience and optimism to those around you.
   - **Example**: During a project setback, focus on identifying and implementing corrective actions rather than dwelling on the issues, which shows resilience and a positive mindset.
2. **Practice Gratitude and Positive Reframing**: Cultivate a habit of gratitude by acknowledging and appreciating the positive aspects of your life and experiences. Use positive reframing to view challenges as opportunities for growth and learning.
   - **Example**: When faced with a setback, remind yourself of the lessons learned and express gratitude for the opportunity to develop new skills or perspectives.
3. **Manage Stress Through Self-Care**: Taking care of your physical and mental well-being can help maintain a positive outlook. Engage in self-care practices such as exercise, mindfulness, and adequate rest to manage stress and enhance resilience.
   - **Example**: Incorporate regular exercise and relaxation techniques into your routine to maintain a balanced and positive mindset, even during stressful times.
4. **Stay Flexible and Adaptable**: Embrace change and remain adaptable in the face of uncertainty. Being open to adjusting your plans and expectations allows you to maintain a positive attitude and effectively manage evolving situations.

- ◦ **Example**: If a planned event is canceled or altered, adapt to the changes with a positive attitude and explore alternative ways to achieve your goals.

5. **Inspire and Motivate Others**: Your positivity and resilience can inspire and motivate those around you. By demonstrating a positive attitude in challenging situations, you encourage others to adopt a similar mindset and approach, strengthening your influence and relationships.

   - ◦ **Example**: As a team leader, maintain a positive and resilient attitude during a project crisis to inspire your team to stay focused and motivated, enhancing overall team performance and cohesion.

Radiating confidence and positivity in social interactions involves projecting assurance without arrogance, exuding warmth and enthusiasm, and maintaining a positive outlook even in challenging situations. By employing these strategies, you can enhance your ability to connect with others, foster meaningful relationships, and positively influence those around you.

Using Compliments and Appreciation to Build Rapport

The Importance of Authentic Compliments and Showing Appreciation to Build Meaningful Connections

Authentic compliments and genuine appreciation are powerful tools in building rapport and fostering meaningful connections. They help establish trust, create positive interactions, and strengthen relationships by making others feel valued and acknowledged. Here's why these elements are crucial:

1. **Fostering Trust and Respect**: When you offer sincere compliments and show appreciation, you demonstrate that you recognize and value the other person's qualities and efforts. This acknowledgment fosters a sense of trust and respect, laying the foundation for a deeper connection.
   - **Example**: Complimenting a colleague on their exceptional presentation skills not only validates their effort but also builds mutual respect and trust in the professional relationship.
2. **Enhancing Positive Interactions**: Authentic compliments and appreciation contribute to a positive atmosphere in interactions. They can uplift the mood, reduce tension, and create a more engaging and pleasant environment for communication.
   - **Example**: Expressing genuine appreciation for a friend's thoughtful gesture or support during a difficult time enhances the positivity of the interaction and strengthens the friendship.
3. **Creating Lasting Impressions**: People remember how they feel when interacting with others. Offering sincere compliments and showing appreciation leaves a lasting positive impression, which can make you more memorable and influential in your personal and professional circles.
   - **Example**: Complimenting a guest speaker on their insightful talk can leave a lasting positive impression and establish you as a thoughtful and engaging participant.

Techniques for Giving Thoughtful, Specific Compliments That Resonate

To ensure that your compliments are meaningful and impactful, consider the following techniques:

1. **Be Genuine and Specific**: Tailor your compliments to the individual and their specific qualities or actions. General or vague compliments can seem insincere, while specific praise shows that you have genuinely noticed and appreciated their unique contributions.
   - **Example**: Instead of saying, "You did a great job," try, "Your detailed analysis in the report was incredibly thorough and insightful, and it significantly helped our team make better decisions."

2. **Focus on Effort and Achievements**: Highlight the effort or achievement behind the compliment rather than focusing solely on personal attributes. This approach shows that you appreciate the hard work and dedication involved, which adds depth to your praise.
   - **Example**: Compliment a team member by saying, "I noticed how much extra time you invested to ensure the project was completed on schedule. Your dedication really made a difference."

3. **Use Positive and Encouraging Language**: Choose words that are enthusiastic and supportive. Positive language can enhance the impact of your compliment and convey a sense of genuine admiration and encouragement.
   - **Example**: Instead of simply saying, "Nice work," you could say, "Your creativity and attention to detail in this project are truly impressive. I'm excited to see what you'll come up with next!"

4. **Timing and Context Matter**: Offer compliments and appreciation at appropriate times and in suitable contexts. Providing feedback when it is relevant and timely increases its effectiveness and shows that you are attentive and considerate.
   - **Example**: Compliment a colleague immediately after they deliver a successful presentation, rather than

waiting until days later, to reinforce the positive impact of their effort.

Why Expressing Gratitude and Appreciation Strengthens Relationships Over Time

Expressing gratitude and appreciation plays a crucial role in nurturing and sustaining relationships. Here's why it is so effective in building and maintaining strong connections:

1. **Strengthening Bonds**: Regular expressions of gratitude and appreciation help reinforce the positive aspects of a relationship. By consistently acknowledging and valuing the efforts and qualities of others, you strengthen the bond and create a more enduring connection.
   - **Example**: Continually showing appreciation for a partner's support and contributions in a relationship reinforces mutual respect and affection, deepening the emotional connection over time.
2. **Encouraging Positive Behavior**: When people receive genuine appreciation, they are more likely to repeat the behaviors or actions that were recognized. This creates a cycle of positive reinforcement and encourages ongoing engagement and contribution.
   - **Example**: A manager who regularly acknowledges their team's hard work fosters a culture of appreciation and motivation, leading to increased productivity and job satisfaction.
3. **Building Emotional Resilience**: Gratitude and appreciation contribute to emotional resilience by fostering a sense of worth and belonging. This emotional support helps individuals cope with challenges and strengthens the overall quality of the relationship.

- ◦ **Example**: Expressing appreciation to a friend during tough times can provide emotional support and enhance their resilience, reinforcing the strength of the friendship.

4. **Creating a Positive Feedback Loop**: When you regularly express gratitude and appreciation, it creates a positive feedback loop. People are more likely to respond in kind, resulting in a reciprocal exchange of positive sentiments and reinforcing the overall quality of interactions.

   - ◦ **Example**: A team leader who consistently shows appreciation for their team's efforts will likely receive positive feedback and increased cooperation in return, creating a more collaborative and supportive work environment.

In summary, using authentic compliments and appreciation effectively is crucial for building and nurturing meaningful relationships. By being genuine, specific, and timely in your praise, and by consistently expressing gratitude, you foster trust, enhance interactions, and strengthen connections over time.

MASTERING BODY LANGUAGE AND NON-VERBAL CUES

The Importance of Body Language in Communication

Understanding How Body Language Often Speaks Louder Than Words

Body language plays a crucial role in communication, often conveying more meaning than the spoken word. While verbal communication can be explicit and direct, body language provides additional context and emotional depth, revealing how we truly feel and react in various situations. Understanding this aspect of communication is essential for effective interpersonal interactions.

1. **Non-Verbal Cues Reveal True Feelings**: Body language can often express emotions and attitudes that words alone might not fully capture. For instance, someone may verbally agree with you, but their body language—such as crossed arms or avoiding eye contact—might indicate disagreement or discomfort.
   - **Example**: During a discussion, if a person is nodding and maintaining eye contact but their arms are crossed tightly, it might suggest that they are not fully open to the conversation despite their verbal agreement.

2. **Body Language Complements or Contradicts Words**: Effective communication requires alignment between verbal and non-verbal messages. Discrepancies between what is said and how it is expressed through body language can lead to confusion or mistrust.
   - **Example**: A manager who verbally praises an employee but avoids eye contact and has a closed posture may cause the employee to question the sincerity of the praise.

3. **Building Rapport and Trust**: Positive body language can enhance rapport and trust between individuals. Open, relaxed gestures and positive facial expressions can create a welcoming atmosphere and facilitate smoother interactions.
   - **Example**: Smiling and leaning slightly forward when conversing with someone can signal warmth and interest, helping to build a positive connection.

The Different Elements of Non-Verbal Communication

Non-verbal communication encompasses several key elements that contribute to how messages are conveyed and interpreted:

1. **Facial Expressions**: The face is one of the most expressive parts of the body, capable of conveying a wide range of emotions including happiness, sadness, anger, and surprise. Facial expressions often provide immediate feedback about our feelings and reactions.
   - **Example**: A genuine smile involves not just the mouth but also the eyes, creating a warm and authentic expression that communicates friendliness and approachability.
2. **Posture**: The way we sit or stand can indicate confidence, openness, or defensiveness. Open and relaxed posture typically suggests comfort and receptiveness, while closed or tense posture might indicate discomfort or resistance.
   - **Example**: Standing with arms open and shoulders relaxed can signal confidence and openness, whereas slouching or crossing arms may suggest insecurity or disinterest.
3. **Gestures**: Hand movements, nods, and other gestures can emphasize or clarify verbal messages. They can also convey emotions or reactions and enhance the expressiveness of communication.
   - **Example**: Using hand gestures to illustrate points during a conversation can help make the message more vivid and engaging, while excessive or erratic gestures may distract from the content.
4. **Tone of Voice**: The tone, pitch, and pace of your voice can greatly influence how your message is perceived. A

warm, steady tone can convey assurance and friendliness, whereas a harsh or monotonous tone may come across as disinterest or irritation.

- ◦ **Example**: Speaking with enthusiasm and varying your tone can make the conversation more engaging and convey genuine interest, while a flat or disinterested tone may signal boredom or disengagement.

How to Become More Aware of Your Own Body Language and the Messages You're Sending

Becoming more aware of your own body language involves self-observation, reflection, and practice. Here are some strategies to enhance your awareness:

1. **Self-Observation**: Pay attention to how you naturally use body language in different situations. Notice your facial expressions, posture, and gestures during conversations and interactions.
   - ◦ **Tip**: Consider recording yourself during practice conversations or presentations to observe and analyze your body language objectively.
2. **Seek Feedback**: Ask trusted friends, colleagues, or mentors for feedback on your body language. They can provide valuable insights into how your non-verbal cues are perceived by others.
   - ◦ **Tip**: Request specific feedback on aspects such as eye contact, posture, and gestures to gain a comprehensive understanding of your body language.
3. **Practice in Front of a Mirror**: Rehearse various interactions or presentations in front of a mirror to become more conscious of your body language. This practice can help you adjust and refine your non-verbal communication.

- **Tip**: Focus on different elements such as maintaining open posture, making appropriate eye contact, and using expressive gestures to enhance your communication effectiveness.

4. **Mindfulness and Reflection**: Develop mindfulness about your emotional state and how it affects your body language. Reflect on how your feelings and attitudes might influence your non-verbal signals.

   - **Tip**: Take a moment before interactions to assess your emotions and consciously adopt a positive and open posture to align with your intended message.

5. **Adjust Based on Context**: Adapt your body language to suit the context and audience of the interaction. Different situations may require varying levels of formality or expressiveness.

   - **Tip**: In formal settings, maintain a professional posture and restrained gestures, while in casual or creative environments, you might use more expressive and relaxed body language.

In summary, understanding and effectively utilizing body language is crucial for enhancing communication and building strong relationships. By becoming more aware of your non-verbal cues and ensuring they align with your verbal messages, you can improve your ability to connect with others, convey your true intentions, and create more meaningful interactions.

Reading and Responding to Non-Verbal Signals

How to Accurately Read Others' Body Language and Interpret Subtle Cues

Understanding and interpreting body language involves more than just observing physical actions; it requires reading subtle cues and understanding their context. Accurate reading of non-verbal signals can provide deeper insights into others' emotions, intentions, and reactions.

1. **Observe Consistently**: Pay attention to body language consistently throughout an interaction, rather than focusing on isolated moments. This helps to understand the overall emotional state and intentions of the other person.
   - **Example**: Notice if someone's posture remains open or closed throughout a conversation. Continuous observation helps discern whether their initial discomfort was an isolated reaction or a consistent attitude.
2. **Look for Clusters of Cues**: Single gestures or expressions can be ambiguous, but clusters of non-verbal signals often provide clearer insights. Look for patterns in facial expressions, gestures, and posture.
   - **Example**: If a person is fidgeting with their hands, avoiding eye contact, and crossing their arms, it may indicate anxiety or discomfort rather than just one isolated cue.
3. **Context Matters**: Always consider the context in which body language occurs. The same gesture might have different meanings depending on the situation, relationship, or cultural norms.

- ◦ **Example**: Leaning in might indicate interest in a conversation, but in a different context, it could be perceived as intrusive.

4. **Facial Expressions**: Facial expressions are powerful indicators of emotions. Subtle changes in expressions, such as slight furrows in the brow or small smiles, can convey feelings that words may not express.
   - ◦ **Example**: A person might smile briefly in response to a compliment but quickly look away, suggesting they are pleased but also modest or uncomfortable with the attention.

5. **Gestures and Posture**: Analyze how people use their hands and posture. Open gestures and relaxed posture typically indicate comfort and openness, while closed or rigid postures may signal resistance or discomfort.
   - ◦ **Example**: A person who keeps their hands in their lap and avoids leaning in may be feeling reserved or hesitant about the discussion.

6. **Tone and Speech Patterns**: Pay attention to how body language interacts with tone and speech patterns. The tone of voice, combined with non-verbal signals, can provide clues about the speaker's true feelings or intentions.
   - ◦ **Example**: A cheerful tone combined with crossed arms might suggest a person is trying to mask their true feelings of frustration or defensiveness.

Techniques for Responding to Non-Verbal Signals to Improve Communication and Connection

Effective communication involves not only reading body language but also responding to it in a way that fosters connection and understanding.

1. **Mirror and Match**: Subtly mirroring the other person's body language can create a sense of rapport and empathy. This technique helps to build trust and make the other person feel understood.
   - **Example**: If someone is leaning forward and nodding, you might do the same in a subtle manner to show engagement and agreement.
2. **Adjust Your Approach**: Modify your own body language in response to the signals you observe. If someone appears closed off, adopt a more open and welcoming posture to encourage them to relax.
   - **Example**: If a person is crossing their arms and leaning back, try adjusting your own posture to be more open and approachable to make them feel more comfortable.
3. **Acknowledge and Address Cues**: If you notice signs of discomfort or distress, address them directly with empathy. This can help alleviate tension and foster better communication.
   - **Example**: If someone looks anxious, acknowledge their feelings by saying, "I notice you seem a bit uncomfortable. Is there something on your mind or something I can do to help?"
4. **Use Positive Reinforcement**: Reinforce positive body language by responding with affirmative gestures and expressions. This can encourage continued open communication and build a positive interaction.
   - **Example**: When someone is making eye contact and nodding in agreement, respond with a smile and affirming words to reinforce their engagement and support.
5. **Create a Comfortable Environment**: Ensure that the physical environment supports open and relaxed body lan-

guage. A comfortable setting can help people feel more at ease and express themselves more freely.

- ◦ **Example**: Arrange seating in a way that allows for face-to-face conversation without barriers, and ensure the setting is conducive to open dialogue.

The Importance of Cultural Awareness in Interpreting Body Language

Cultural differences play a significant role in how body language is expressed and interpreted. Being aware of these differences is essential for accurate communication and avoiding misunderstandings.

1. **Cultural Norms Vary**: Body language norms vary widely between cultures. For instance, eye contact may be seen as a sign of confidence in some cultures, while in others, it might be considered disrespectful.
   - ◦ **Example**: In many Western cultures, direct eye contact is encouraged during conversation, whereas in some Asian cultures, prolonged eye contact might be avoided to show respect.
2. **Gesture Meanings Differ**: Certain gestures can have different meanings across cultures. A gesture that is considered polite in one culture might be interpreted as rude or inappropriate in another.
   - ◦ **Example**: The thumbs-up gesture is generally positive in Western cultures but can be offensive in some Middle Eastern countries.
3. **Contextual Understanding**: Always consider the cultural context when interpreting body language. What is acceptable behavior in one culture may not be in another, and

understanding these nuances helps in making accurate interpretations.

- ◦ **Example**: In a business setting, understanding that some cultures value formality and restraint in body language, while others might favor a more relaxed and informal approach, can improve communication effectiveness.

4. **Ask and Learn**: If you are unsure about specific cultural norms, it's okay to ask politely or seek information about cultural practices. Demonstrating a willingness to understand and respect cultural differences fosters positive relationships.

- ◦ **Tip**: Engage in cultural competence training or consult resources on cross-cultural communication to enhance your understanding and skills.

In conclusion, mastering the art of reading and responding to non-verbal signals involves keen observation, contextual understanding, and adaptability. By paying attention to body language, responding appropriately, and being mindful of cultural differences, you can enhance your communication skills and build more meaningful and effective connections with others.

Using Open and Inviting Body Language

Techniques for Projecting Openness, Approachability, and Confidence

Effective body language can significantly enhance your interactions by making you appear more open, approachable, and confident. Mastering these techniques helps foster positive relationships and encourages others to engage with you more freely.

1. **Maintain an Open Posture**: An open posture signifies receptiveness and willingness to engage. To project openness:
   - **Stand or Sit with an Uncrossed Posture**: Keep your arms relaxed and avoid crossing them over your chest, which can appear defensive or closed-off.
   - **Orient Your Body Toward Others**: Face the person you're interacting with directly. This signals that you are fully engaged and interested in the conversation.
2. **Use Welcoming Gestures**: Gestures can communicate warmth and approachability. Incorporate these practices:
   - **Open-Handed Gestures**: Use gestures that show your palms or keep your hands open. This indicates transparency and friendliness.
   - **Leaning Slightly Forward**: Lean in slightly during conversations to show attentiveness and interest. This gesture conveys that you are actively engaged and attentive.
3. **Make and Maintain Eye Contact**: Eye contact is a crucial component of non-verbal communication. To use eye contact effectively:
   - **Establish Eye Contact**: Look at the person you are speaking with to show that you are present and focused on them.
   - **Balance Eye Contact**: Maintain eye contact without staring. Break it occasionally to avoid making the other person uncomfortable and to show that you are genuinely engaged.
4. **Smile Warmly**: A genuine smile can create a positive atmosphere and make you appear more approachable.
   - **Use a Natural Smile**: Ensure your smile reaches your eyes, creating a warm and inviting expression. Avoid forced or mechanical smiles, which can seem insincere.

5. **Exude Confident Posture**: Confidence can be communicated through your posture. To project confidence:
    - **Stand Tall**: Maintain a straight but relaxed posture. Avoid slouching or hunching over, which can convey uncertainty or lack of confidence.
    - **Use Firm, Controlled Movements**: Movements should be purposeful and deliberate, rather than erratic or hesitant. This demonstrates self-assuredness and control.

How to Use Gestures, Eye Contact, and Posture to Make Others Feel Comfortable

To make others feel comfortable and valued, tailor your body language to create an inviting and supportive environment:

1. **Gestures**:
    - **Encouraging Gestures**: Use gestures that invite interaction, such as nodding or open-handed gestures. These indicate that you are receptive to their input and willing to engage.
    - **Affirmative Gestures**: Simple gestures like a thumbs-up or a gentle wave can reinforce positive communication and encourage openness.
2. **Eye Contact**:
    - **Reassuring Eye Contact**: Maintain eye contact to build trust and show that you are attentive. Avoiding eye contact can be perceived as disinterest or evasiveness.
    - **Use Warm Expressions**: Pair eye contact with a smile or a nod to convey warmth and reassurance, making others feel valued and heard.
3. **Posture**:

- ◦ **Encourage Engagement**: Position your body to face the other person directly, and avoid barriers like desks or tables that can create physical distance.
- ◦ **Relaxed Posture**: Adopt a relaxed but engaged posture, avoiding rigid or overly formal stances that can create a barrier.

Avoiding Closed-Off or Defensive Body Language That Can Create Barriers to Connection

Certain body language signals can create barriers to effective communication and hinder the development of rapport. Being aware of and avoiding these signals helps to maintain a positive interaction:

1. **Crossed Arms**: Crossing your arms over your chest can appear defensive or closed-off. Instead, keep your arms relaxed at your sides or use open-handed gestures to convey openness.
    - ◦ **Alternative**: Use arm gestures that invite interaction or support, such as placing your hands on the table or making gentle, open gestures.
2. **Avoiding Eye Contact**: Not making eye contact can be interpreted as disinterest, discomfort, or even dishonesty. Ensure you make consistent eye contact, but avoid staring, which can be uncomfortable.
    - ◦ **Alternative**: Look at the person while speaking and listening, and periodically break eye contact to avoid creating pressure.
3. **Rigid Posture**: A rigid or tense posture can signal anxiety or discomfort. Instead, adopt a relaxed yet engaged posture that reflects confidence and approachability.

- ◦ **Alternative**: Relax your shoulders and adopt a slightly forward-leaning position to convey engagement and interest.

4. **Turning Away or Creating Physical Barriers**: Turning your body away or placing objects between you and the other person can create a sense of separation. Ensure that your body is oriented toward the person, and avoid physical barriers whenever possible.
   - ◦ **Alternative**: Position yourself to face the other person directly and minimize obstacles that could create distance.

5. **Fidgeting or Distracted Behavior**: Fidgeting or appearing distracted can suggest a lack of interest or respect. Focus on the interaction and minimize distracting behaviors to show that you are fully engaged.
   - ◦ **Alternative**: Maintain a steady posture and give your full attention to the conversation, demonstrating that you value the interaction.

By employing open and inviting body language, you create an environment conducive to effective communication and connection. This approach not only enhances your interactions but also fosters positive relationships and helps you build stronger, more meaningful connections with others.

WINNING PEOPLE OVER WITH PERSUASION, NOT MANIPULAT

Persuasion is a powerful tool that can help you win people over, build connections, and influence others in a positive, ethical way. However, for persuasion to be effective and long-lasting, it must be grounded in respect, integrity, and mutual benefit, as opposed to manipulation, which erodes trust and damages relationships. In this chapter, we will explore the difference between persuasion and manipulation, focusing on ethical persuasion techniques. These techniques involve key psychological principles and the ability to craft arguments that align with others' values while maintaining honesty and integrity.

Understanding the Difference Between Influence and Manipulation

In the realm of communication and relationships, distinguishing between influence and manipulation is crucial. Both can affect people's decisions and behaviors, but they operate on different principles and have vastly different impacts on relationships and trust.

Defining Ethical Influence Versus Manipulation

Ethical Influence:

- **Definition**: Ethical influence involves guiding others' decisions or behaviors through transparent, honest, and respectful means. It focuses on mutual benefit and respects the autonomy and well-being of all parties involved.
- **Characteristics**:
    - **Transparency**: The intentions and methods are clear and open.
    - **Respect**: Acknowledges and values the other person's perspectives and autonomy.
    - **Honesty**: Uses truthful and accurate information to inform and persuade.

Manipulation:

- **Definition**: Manipulation involves exerting control or influence over others in a deceptive, coercive, or self-serving manner. It often seeks to benefit the manipulator at the expense of the manipulated individual's best interests.
- **Characteristics**:
    - **Deception**: Involves misleading or concealing true intentions or information.
    - **Coercion**: Applies pressure or tactics that undermine the other person's ability to make an informed choice.

- **Self-Interest**: Prioritizes the manipulator's goals over the well-being of others.

How Manipulation Erodes Trust and Damages Relationships, While Influence Builds Mutual Respect

Impact of Manipulation:

- **Erosion of Trust**: Manipulation undermines trust by engaging in deceitful practices. When individuals discover they have been manipulated, they often feel betrayed and lose confidence in the manipulator.
- **Damage to Relationships**: Manipulation can create rifts in relationships as it fosters feelings of betrayal and exploitation. The manipulative behavior may lead to long-term damage, making it challenging to restore trust.
- **Emotional Fallout**: Victims of manipulation may experience frustration, anger, and a diminished sense of self-worth, as their autonomy and decision-making are undermined.

Impact of Ethical Influence:

- **Building Mutual Respect**: Ethical influence fosters an environment of mutual respect and collaboration. It involves listening to others, understanding their needs, and working together towards common goals.
- **Strengthening Trust**: By being transparent and honest, ethical influence strengthens trust. People are more likely to value and support individuals who are genuine and respectful.
- **Positive Relationship Outcomes**: Ethical influence enhances relationships by promoting open communication

and shared understanding. It leads to more sustainable and positive interactions.

Examples of Healthy Versus Unhealthy Persuasion Tactics

Healthy Persuasion Tactics:

1. **Active Listening**: Engaging in active listening to understand the other person's perspective before presenting your own ideas.
   - *Example*: In a team meeting, actively listening to colleagues' concerns before suggesting a new project approach.
2. **Honest Communication**: Being straightforward about your intentions and providing truthful information.
   - *Example*: Explaining the benefits and potential drawbacks of a proposed change in a clear and honest manner.
3. **Empathy and Understanding**: Demonstrating empathy by acknowledging and addressing the emotional and practical needs of others.
   - *Example*: Offering support and understanding to a colleague struggling with a heavy workload, while discussing possible solutions.
4. **Mutual Benefit**: Focusing on solutions or proposals that benefit all parties involved.
   - *Example*: Proposing a flexible work schedule that accommodates both personal needs and organizational goals.

Unhealthy Persuasion Tactics:

1. **Deception**: Providing misleading or incomplete information to manipulate someone's decision.
   - *Example*: Withholding key details about a product's limitations to make a sale.
2. **Pressure Tactics**: Using high-pressure strategies to coerce someone into making a decision they're uncomfortable with.
   - *Example*: Applying excessive urgency to force a quick decision on a contract without allowing adequate time for consideration.
3. **Guilt-Tripping**: Using emotional manipulation to make someone feel guilty or obligated to act in a certain way.
   - *Example*: Imposing undue guilt on a friend for not attending an event, despite their valid reasons for absence.
4. **Exploiting Vulnerabilities**: Taking advantage of someone's weaknesses or insecurities to influence their behavior.
   - *Example*: Using a person's financial struggles to convince them to make a decision that benefits you.

In summary, ethical influence is about guiding and persuading with integrity and respect, aiming for mutually beneficial outcomes and fostering positive relationships. Manipulation, on the other hand, involves deceitful or coercive tactics that damage trust and harm relationships. Recognizing and applying these principles can significantly impact the quality of your interactions and the strength of your relationships.

Ethical Persuasion Techniques

Ethical persuasion is about convincing others while respecting their autonomy, emotions, and priorities. Unlike manipulation, which deceives or pressures people into making decisions that might not be in their best interest, ethical persuasion is about transparency, mutual respect, and finding solutions that work for all parties involved. Understanding how to use ethical persuasion can strengthen your ability to win people over and create long-lasting, trusting relationships.

One of the most influential voices in understanding the dynamics of persuasion is Dr. Robert Cialdini, a social psychologist whose research outlined several principles of persuasion. Let's dive into three core principles: reciprocity, scarcity, and consistency.

The Principles of Reciprocity, Scarcity, and Consistency in Persuasion

1. Reciprocity: The Power of Giving and Receiving

The principle of reciprocity is based on the idea that people tend to feel obligated to return a favor when someone does something for them. This instinctual response is rooted in social norms and plays a significant role in interpersonal relationships and persuasion.

- **How Reciprocity Works**: When you offer help, provide useful information, or give something of value to others without expecting anything in return, they are likely to feel a sense of indebtedness and will be more inclined to help or support you in the future.
- **Example in Persuasion**: In a business setting, offering a free resource or valuable advice to a potential client can create goodwill. When you later approach them with a proposal or request, they are more likely to listen and respond positively, as they feel a sense of reciprocity.

· **Ethical Use of Reciprocity**: It's important to use this principle with genuine intent. If you give solely for the purpose of expecting something in return, it can come across as manipulative. Ethical reciprocity involves giving because it's beneficial to others and because you genuinely want to help.

2. Scarcity: Creating a Sense of Urgency

Scarcity is the idea that people are more likely to value and desire things that are perceived as limited or hard to obtain. When something is scarce or available for a limited time, people fear missing out, which makes them more motivated to act.

· **How Scarcity Works**: When you highlight the uniqueness or limited availability of an opportunity, product, or idea, it creates a sense of urgency. People tend to act more quickly when they believe they might lose an opportunity.

· **Example in Persuasion**: A real estate agent might tell a potential buyer that several other offers have already been made on a property. This creates a sense of urgency and scarcity, making the buyer more likely to take action before the opportunity slips away.

· **Ethical Use of Scarcity**: It's essential to be truthful about scarcity. If you fabricate scarcity or create false urgency, people may feel manipulated when they discover the reality. Ethical scarcity focuses on genuinely limited opportunities or resources, making sure that any sense of urgency is based on facts.

3. Consistency: Aligning Actions with Beliefs

The principle of consistency taps into people's desire to act in a way that aligns with their previous commitments, beliefs, and values. When people publicly commit to something, they feel internal pressure to stick to that commitment to maintain consistency in their behavior.

- **How Consistency Works**: If someone agrees with your initial proposal or idea, they are more likely to follow through with future actions that are consistent with that stance. This is especially powerful if they make their commitments publicly or in writing.
- **Example in Persuasion**: A manager might ask an employee if they value teamwork and collaboration. Once the employee agrees, the manager could later ask them to participate in a collaborative project, tapping into the principle of consistency since the employee has already expressed the importance of teamwork.
- **Ethical Use of Consistency**: Use this principle to encourage people to make commitments that align with their values and beliefs, rather than coercing them into agreements they are unsure of. Ethical consistency involves helping others stay true to their own standards and ideals, not exploiting their commitment for self-serving purposes.

How to Craft Compelling Arguments That Align with Others' Values and Priorities

One of the most effective ways to persuade ethically is by understanding and aligning your arguments with the values and priorities of the person you are trying to influence. People are more likely to be persuaded when they see how your ideas align with their existing beliefs, goals, and needs.

1. Know Your Audience:

The first step in crafting a persuasive argument is understanding who you're trying to influence. This involves actively listening to their needs, concerns, and values. Tailoring your message to resonate with their priorities shows that you respect their perspective and are genuinely interested in helping them achieve their goals.

- **Example**: If you're persuading a team to adopt a new project management tool, you should first understand their pain points. Are they struggling with efficiency or collaboration? Then, frame your argument around how the tool addresses those specific concerns, highlighting its potential to make their work easier and more productive.

2. Appeal to Shared Values:

People are more likely to be persuaded by arguments that align with their core values. When you demonstrate that your proposal is consistent with values that are important to the person you're addressing, they will be more receptive.

- **Example**: If you know that someone values sustainability, emphasize how your solution or product aligns with environmental responsibility. Highlighting shared values creates a sense of unity and trust, making persuasion easier.

3. Use Clear and Logical Arguments:

Persuasion is most effective when it is grounded in logic and evidence. Present your ideas in a clear, well-structured manner that leads the other person through a logical progression of thought. Avoid using emotional manipulation or fallacies that can undermine your credibility.

- **Example**: If you're proposing a new strategy at work, provide concrete data, research, and case studies that support your argument. Demonstrating that your ideas are well-reasoned and backed by evidence makes it easier for others to get on board.

4. Incorporate Emotional Appeal, But Avoid Exploitation:

While logic is important, emotions also play a crucial role in decision-making. Ethical persuasion involves appealing to emotions without exploiting or manipulating them. Share stories, examples, or testimonials that evoke positive emotions such as inspiration, hope, or empathy.

- **Example**: In a nonprofit setting, you might share a personal story about how a donation has changed someone's life. This helps potential donors feel a deeper emotional connection to the cause, motivating them to contribute without feeling pressured or manipulated.

Why Persuasion Should Always Be Rooted in Honesty, Integrity, and Mutual Benefit

Ethical persuasion must always be based on honesty, integrity, and mutual benefit to ensure long-term trust and positive relationships. When you persuade others, your goal should be to create outcomes that benefit both parties. This approach not only helps you achieve your goals but also builds respect, trust, and credibility over time.

1. Honesty as the Foundation of Persuasion:

Honesty is a non-negotiable aspect of ethical persuasion. People will quickly lose trust in someone who is dishonest, and once trust is broken, it's challenging to regain. Being upfront about the benefits, risks, and potential outcomes of a situation fosters transparency and helps establish long-term trust.

- **Example**: If you're selling a product, be transparent about both its strengths and limitations. A customer who knows the full picture will feel more confident in their decision and trust you as a reliable source.

2. Integrity in Action:

Integrity means staying true to your values and principles even when it's difficult. In the context of persuasion, it means avoiding shortcuts or tactics that compromise your ethics just to get what you want. Upholding your integrity allows you to build lasting relationships based on respect and trust.

- **Example**: A business leader might refuse to exaggerate performance metrics to persuade investors. Instead, they present honest, realistic projections, knowing that long-term success depends on maintaining integrity.

3. Mutual Benefit for Long-Lasting Relationships:

Persuasion should not be about convincing someone to do something that benefits only you. Instead, it should be about finding solutions that are mutually beneficial, creating a win-win situation. This builds goodwill and ensures that relationships are not only persuasive in the short term but also enduring over time.

- **Example**: In negotiation, seek to understand what the other party values most and offer compromises that ensure both parties walk away feeling satisfied with the outcome. This approach promotes collaboration and fosters long-term partnerships.

In conclusion, ethical persuasion is an essential skill for building trust, relationships, and influence without crossing the line into manipulation. By understanding and applying the principles of reciprocity, scarcity, and consistency, as well as crafting compelling, value-aligned arguments, you can ethically persuade others while fostering long-term respect and mutual benefit.

Aligning Your Goals with Others' Desires

Persuasion is most powerful when it creates alignment between your goals and the desires of those you are trying to influence. By finding common ground and understanding the motivations and needs of others, you can present your ideas in a way that resonates more deeply. This approach helps foster cooperation and mutual benefit, rather than creating tension or resistance. Key to this process is the use of empathy and open communication, allowing for a connection that avoids coercion and focuses on shared goals.

Techniques for Finding Common Ground and Aligning Your Objectives with the Needs of Others

The ability to find common ground and align your goals with those of others is essential for successful persuasion. The more you can tailor your arguments and solutions to meet both your needs and theirs, the more likely you are to create positive outcomes for everyone involved.

1. Active Listening to Understand Needs and Priorities:

One of the most effective techniques for finding common ground is active listening. This means truly focusing on the other person's words, emotions, and underlying motivations without interrupting or rushing to respond. By understanding their needs and concerns, you can position your goals in a way that aligns with what they value most.

- **Example**: If you're working on a team project and want to propose a new idea, start by asking your colleagues about their main concerns or goals. By listening to their responses, you can shape your pitch to show how your idea addresses their specific challenges, making it easier for them to support you.

2. Framing Your Objectives to Address Mutual Benefits:

Once you understand the needs and desires of others, you can frame your objectives in terms of mutual benefits. This technique allows you to demonstrate how your goals not only serve your own interests but also help the other person or group achieve theirs.

· **Example**: If you're negotiating a business deal, rather than focusing solely on what you want, emphasize how the deal will benefit both parties. Highlight the advantages, such as increased profitability for them or access to new markets, making it clear that the success of the deal is a win-win scenario.

3. Collaborative Problem-Solving:

Rather than imposing your solution on others, involve them in the process of finding a solution that works for both sides. Collaborative problem-solving encourages others to contribute their ideas and helps ensure that the final outcome is something that everyone can support.

· **Example**: In a workplace conflict, instead of dictating a resolution, invite the other person to share their perspective and propose solutions. Together, you can brainstorm ways to resolve the issue in a way that meets both your needs, fostering a sense of shared ownership over the outcome.

The Role of Empathy in Persuasive Communication

Empathy is a crucial component of persuasive communication because it allows you to understand and connect with the emotions, desires, and concerns of the person you are trying to influence. By putting yourself in their shoes, you can communicate in a way that speaks to their inner motivations, making your argument more compelling and meaningful.

1. Understanding Emotional Drivers:

Every decision people make is influenced by a combination of logic and emotion. By using empathy to understand the emotional drivers behind someone's choices, you can craft messages that resonate more deeply and are more likely to persuade.

- **Example**: A manager trying to motivate an employee to take on a challenging project might recognize that the employee feels overwhelmed by their workload. Rather than simply assigning the task, the manager can acknowledge their stress, offer support, and present the project as an opportunity for growth and skill-building, addressing both practical and emotional concerns.

2. Building Emotional Connection:

People are more likely to be influenced by someone they feel connected to. Empathy helps you build rapport and emotional connection, making it easier to communicate persuasively. When people feel understood, they are more open to considering new ideas or perspectives.

- **Example**: In a sales context, if a customer expresses hesitation about making a purchase, instead of pushing them to buy, the salesperson can empathize with their concerns, perhaps relating to budget or uncertainty. By acknowledging and validating their feelings, the salesperson can then provide reassurance or alternatives that align with the customer's emotional needs.

3. Tailoring Your Communication Style:

Empathy also allows you to adapt your communication style based on the other person's preferences and emotions. Some people may respond better to detailed, data-driven arguments, while others may be more persuaded by personal stories or emotional appeals. Understanding these preferences helps you connect more effectively.

- **Example**: If you're giving a presentation to a group of investors, and you know they value data, you might lead with financial forecasts and statistical evidence. On the other hand, if your audience is more emotionally driven, sharing a personal success story or customer testimonial might resonate more strongly.

How to Influence Without Coercion by Tapping into Shared Goals and Motivations

Influence becomes much more effective when it is based on shared goals and motivations, rather than coercion or pressure. Coercion tends to create resistance and undermine trust, whereas influence rooted in mutual understanding fosters collaboration and long-term success.

1. Aligning Your Vision with Others' Motivations:

When you align your goals with the core motivations of others, you create a sense of shared purpose. People are much more likely to be influenced when they see that your goals overlap with their own, and that working together can lead to mutual success.

- **Example**: A team leader trying to implement a new process might explain how it will streamline workflow and make everyone's jobs easier, rather than simply ordering the team to adopt it. By showing how the new process aligns with the team's desire for efficiency and reduced workload, the leader can gain their cooperation without forcing the issue.

2. Using Positive Reinforcement:

Positive reinforcement is a powerful way to influence others without using coercion. Recognizing and rewarding progress, contributions, and shared achievements reinforces the sense that working together is mutually beneficial and helps build trust over time.

- **Example**: In a collaborative project, offering praise and acknowledging individual contributions can motivate others to stay engaged and continue working toward the common goal. Positive reinforcement helps people feel valued and more willing to align their efforts with the overall objective.

3. Highlighting Long-Term Benefits:

When influencing others, it's important to emphasize the long-term benefits of aligning with your goals. Often, people resist change because they are focused on short-term inconveniences or uncertainties. By demonstrating how aligning with your objectives will lead to greater rewards or benefits over time, you can reduce resistance and encourage cooperation.

- **Example**: A manager implementing new software might face initial pushback from the team due to the learning curve. By highlighting how the software will save time and reduce errors in the long run, the manager can help the team see the future benefits, making them more willing to adopt the change without feeling coerced.

4. Respecting Autonomy:

True influence respects the autonomy and independence of the other party. Rather than pressuring or manipulating someone into agreeing with you, give them the freedom to make their own decisions. When people feel that they are in control of their choices, they are more likely to embrace your ideas willingly.

- **Example**: If you're trying to get a colleague to support a new initiative, present your case clearly and respectfully, then give them space to consider it without pressing for an immediate decision. This shows respect for their autonomy and can lead to a more genuine, positive alignment with your goals.

By using these techniques for aligning your goals with others' desires, you can create a persuasive dynamic that is rooted in empathy, mutual understanding, and respect. Whether in personal relationships, professional collaborations, or broader negotiations, the ability to influence others in a way that respects their needs and motivations can lead to more successful, harmonious, and lasting outcomes. This ethical approach to influence allows you to build meaningful connections without resorting to coercion, ultimately fostering an environment of cooperation, trust, and shared success.

THE POWER OF AUTHENTICITY – BEING YOURSELF WHILE B

Authenticity has become one of the most sought-after traits in personal and professional relationships. In a world where people often feel pressured to conform to certain expectations or ideals, those who embrace and project their true selves stand out. Authenticity is not just about being honest with others; it's about being true to yourself. When you allow your genuine personality to shine through, you build relationships based on trust, respect, and mutual understanding. Authenticity is a cornerstone for developing deep and lasting connections, and it plays a vital role in influencing others.

Why Authenticity Matters in Relationships

Authenticity is the foundation upon which meaningful relationships are built. When people interact with someone who is genuine, they can feel it. Authenticity fosters a sense of trust because it communicates that you are not hiding behind a mask or trying to deceive others. People are naturally drawn to those who are open, honest, and consistent in their words and actions, making it easier to form deep and lasting connections.

1. Building Trust Through Authenticity:

Trust is a critical component of any successful relationship, whether personal or professional. People are more likely to trust someone who is authentic because authenticity signals honesty and integrity. When you are open about your thoughts, feelings, and intentions, others feel comfortable reciprocating, creating a foundation of trust that can withstand challenges and disagreements.

- **Example**: In a business setting, a leader who acknowledges both their strengths and limitations, rather than pretending to know all the answers, fosters trust among their team. By being authentic, they show that they value transparency and are open to collaboration, which encourages the team to be more open and engaged.

2. Deeper Emotional Connections:

Authenticity allows for deeper emotional connections because it encourages vulnerability. When you are willing to be vulnerable and show your true self, others feel more comfortable doing the same. This openness creates a bond that goes beyond surface-level interactions, leading to relationships that are built on mutual understanding and emotional depth.

- **Example**: In a friendship, being authentic about your struggles and fears can lead to a more meaningful relationship. Instead of keeping conversations superficial, opening up about your true experiences allows your friend to empathize with you and offer genuine support, strengthening the connection.

3. Consistency and Integrity:

People are more likely to trust and respect someone who is consistent in their words and actions. Authenticity ensures that you act in alignment with your values and beliefs, which creates a sense of reliability. When others see that you remain true to yourself in different situations, they are more likely to respect your opinions and decisions.

- **Example**: A colleague who consistently behaves in line with their stated values, whether in the office or during client meetings, demonstrates integrity. Others can trust that this person will act ethically and be dependable, making them someone people want to work with and support.

The Risks of Trying to Be Someone You're Not

While authenticity has many benefits, the opposite – trying to be someone you're not – carries significant risks. People can often sense when someone is being inauthentic, and it can undermine trust and damage relationships. Whether it's pretending to share the same interests as someone else or altering your personality to fit into a particular group, being inauthentic comes with consequences.

1. Loss of Trust:

When people discover that you've been presenting a false version of yourself, it can lead to a loss of trust. If you're trying to fit in by pretending to be something you're not, others may eventually see through the façade, making them question your honesty and reliability.

- **Example**: A manager who pretends to be an expert in a subject they know little about may lose credibility when their lack of knowledge is revealed. Once trust is broken, it can be difficult to regain, and the relationship may suffer as a result.

2. Emotional Exhaustion:

Constantly trying to be someone you're not is emotionally draining. It takes a lot of effort to maintain a façade, and over time, this can lead to burnout and dissatisfaction. Authenticity, on the other hand, allows you to be at ease with who you are, reducing the mental and emotional strain that comes with pretending.

- **Example**: If you're constantly trying to fit in with a group by adopting their behaviors and interests, you may eventually feel disconnected from your true self. This emotional exhaustion can lead to feelings of frustration or resentment, ultimately damaging your well-being and the relationships you're trying to cultivate.

3. Weakening of Relationships:

Inauthentic behavior prevents you from forming deep, meaningful relationships. When you're not being yourself, it's hard for others to get to know the real you. As a result, the connections you build may be shallow or short-lived, as they are based on a false version of yourself.

- **Example**: In a romantic relationship, if one partner is constantly trying to be what they think the other wants, rather than being themselves, the relationship may struggle to grow. True intimacy and connection can only be built on a foundation of honesty and authenticity.

Why Authenticity is Essential for Building Influence

Authenticity is not only important for forming strong relationships, but it is also a critical component of building influence. People are more likely to be influenced by someone they trust and respect, and authenticity plays a key role in earning that trust. When you are genuine in your interactions, others are more inclined to listen to you, value your opinions, and follow your lead.

1. Authenticity Enhances Credibility:

To be influential, people must see you as credible. Authenticity contributes to your credibility by showing that you are honest, transparent, and true to your values. When others believe that you are acting with integrity, they are more likely to take your words and actions seriously.

· **Example**: A leader who is authentic in their communication and decision-making will earn the trust of their team. Employees are more likely to follow a leader who is consistent in their values and actions, knowing that they can rely on them to be fair and honest.

2. Genuine Leaders Inspire Loyalty:

Authentic leaders inspire loyalty because they create an environment where people feel valued and understood. When leaders are open about their values, beliefs, and intentions, they foster a sense of trust and respect that encourages others to be loyal to them and their vision.

· **Example**: A leader who shares their personal journey, including the challenges and failures they've faced, shows vulnerability and humanity. This authenticity can inspire employees to feel more connected to the leader and more invested in the success of the organization.

3. People Respond Positively to Authenticity:

Authenticity is magnetic. People are naturally drawn to those who are real and genuine because it creates a sense of comfort and trust. When you are authentic, you make others feel safe and respected, which makes it easier to build rapport and influence them.

· **Example**: In a networking situation, someone who is authentic about their passions and interests is more likely to attract like-minded individuals. This honesty creates opportunities for genuine connections, which can lead to stronger relationships and greater influence.

How People Respond Positively to Those Who Are Genuine and Transparent

Being authentic in your interactions not only benefits you but also has a positive impact on those around you. When you are genuine and transparent, you create an environment of openness and trust that encourages others to do the same. People respond positively to authenticity because it signals that you are trustworthy, approachable, and relatable.

1. Encouraging Openness and Vulnerability:

When you are authentic, you set the stage for others to be open and vulnerable as well. This creates a safe space for honest communication, where people feel comfortable sharing their thoughts, feelings, and ideas without fear of judgment.

- **Example**: In a team meeting, a leader who is honest about their concerns or uncertainties about a project encourages the team to share their own perspectives and challenges. This openness leads to more productive discussions and problem-solving.

2. Building Mutual Respect:

Authenticity fosters mutual respect because it shows that you are willing to be honest and transparent, even when it's difficult. People respect those who are true to themselves and who have the courage to be vulnerable in their interactions.

- **Example**: In a friendship, if one person is authentic about their feelings, even when they are difficult or uncomfortable to express, the other person is likely to appreciate their honesty and reciprocate with the same level of openness and respect.

3. Creating Meaningful Connections:

People are more likely to form meaningful connections with those who are authentic. When you are genuine, you allow others to see the real you, which helps build deeper, more meaningful relationships. These connections are based on mutual understanding and trust, rather than on pretense or superficiality.

- **Example**: In a networking event, someone who talks openly about their career struggles and successes is more likely to connect with others on a personal level than someone who only shares their achievements. This authenticity leads to more genuine, lasting relationships.

Authenticity is a powerful tool for building trust, forming deeper connections, and influencing others. By embracing your true self and being transparent in your interactions, you not only improve the quality of your relationships but also increase your ability to lead, inspire, and persuade others.

Strategies for Being Genuine Without Oversharing

Being genuine is about striking the right balance between honesty and discretion. While authenticity is vital for building trust and deepening relationships, oversharing can be counterproductive, especially in professional or delicate situations. Knowing how much to reveal, when to share, and how to maintain appropriate boundaries ensures that your authenticity is received positively, without risking your professionalism or comfort. Below are strategies for being genuine while maintaining the right level of personal boundaries.

1. Balancing Honesty with Discretion: When and How Much to Share

The key to being authentic without oversharing is understanding the context of your interactions and recognizing when certain levels of transparency are appropriate. While it's important to be honest, that doesn't mean you need to disclose every personal detail in every situation. Practicing selective vulnerability allows you to show your true self without overwhelming others with unnecessary information.

a. Assess the Relationship:

Consider the depth of your relationship with the person you're interacting with. Close friends or family may expect a higher level of openness compared to acquaintances or coworkers. In casual or professional contexts, it's better to start with a moderate level of sharing and increase it as the relationship deepens.

- **Example**: In a work meeting, it's appropriate to be open about challenges with a project but unnecessary to share personal frustrations that are unrelated. With close friends, you can be more candid about your emotions.

b. Understand the Context:

It's essential to match your level of openness with the situation. While being authentic is encouraged, context dictates how much personal information is suitable. In professional settings, staying focused on relevant information helps you maintain credibility without appearing unprofessional.

· **Example**: During a job interview, you may express genuine enthusiasm for the role and share a personal story about your passion for the industry, but avoid discussing unrelated aspects of your personal life, such as family drama or health issues.

c. Ask Yourself: Is It Necessary?:

Before sharing, ask yourself if the information you're about to disclose adds value to the conversation or connection. Does it help others understand your perspective or situation better, or is it an unnecessary detail? If it's not relevant or helpful, it's probably best to keep it to yourself.

· **Example**: When discussing challenges at work with a colleague, it may be helpful to share how you're managing stress in a healthy way, but unnecessary to discuss unrelated personal hardships unless they directly impact the situation.

2. Techniques for Being Open and Vulnerable Without Crossing Personal Boundaries

Authenticity doesn't require you to open up completely in every interaction. It's possible to be vulnerable without sharing every detail of your personal life, and doing so can help you maintain control over your own boundaries while still being genuine.

a. Share Selectively:

Vulnerability is powerful when it's used intentionally. You can be honest about your emotions or experiences while keeping certain aspects private. This allows you to be open without feeling exposed or uncomfortable later on. Selective vulnerability is about choosing to share things that are relevant to the situation and that contribute to deeper understanding.

- **Example**: If you're leading a team and going through a personal struggle, you can express that you're facing some challenges without going into detail. Sharing that you're dealing with something personal can elicit empathy and understanding from your team without making them feel uncomfortable or burdened.

b. Use Boundaries to Protect Your Comfort:

Being authentic doesn't mean you have to reveal everything. It's okay to set boundaries around what you are and aren't willing to share. If someone asks a question you're uncomfortable answering, it's fine to politely decline or redirect the conversation.

- **Example**: If a coworker asks about your weekend and you experienced something personal you don't want to disclose, you can keep the conversation light by sharing a small positive detail instead. "It was relaxing, and I spent some time catching up on my favorite book" is enough to maintain authenticity without oversharing.

c. Focus on Feelings, Not Details:

One way to express vulnerability without oversharing is to focus on your emotions rather than the specifics of the situation. This allows you to be honest about how something is affecting you without getting into the weeds of personal details.

- **Example**: In a mentoring relationship, you might share how you've felt overwhelmed or uncertain in your career at times without going into every personal circumstance that contributed to that feeling. Focusing on the emotions keeps the conversation genuine without crossing personal boundaries.

3. How to Practice Authenticity in a Professional Context Without Compromising Professionalism

In professional settings, the challenge of authenticity lies in balancing your true self with the standards of the workplace. While openness and honesty can help build trust and rapport in a professional environment, maintaining professionalism is key to ensuring that your authenticity is respected.

a. Maintain Professional Boundaries:

Even when being authentic, it's crucial to maintain a clear boundary between your personal and professional life. Sharing personal experiences that relate to the task or goal at hand can be valuable, but always ensure your disclosures remain appropriate for the setting.

- **Example**: If you're discussing a challenge in a professional context, you can share your personal learning experience without oversharing personal details. For instance, saying, "I've faced similar challenges in my career and found that focusing on clear communication helped," is effective without revealing unnecessary personal details.

b. Be Transparent About Your Intentions:

In the workplace, authenticity can be expressed through transparent communication. If you're faced with difficult decisions or challenges, being upfront about your thought process helps others trust your motives. This doesn't require sharing all your personal reasons, but it does involve being clear about your professional priorities.

- **Example**: If you're making a tough decision that affects your team, explaining the reasoning behind your choice can demonstrate authenticity. You might say, "I've had to weigh several factors, and this decision feels best for the team's long-term success," without delving into personal considerations that don't impact the team directly.

c. Share Personal Stories that Highlight Values:

In professional settings, sharing stories that reveal your values rather than your personal life can help you connect with others while maintaining professionalism. These stories allow you to convey who you are at your core, without delving into overly personal territory.

- **Example**: If you're in a leadership role, sharing a story about how you overcame a challenge in a way that reflects your values—like persistence or integrity—shows authenticity while still keeping the focus on professional development.

d. Emphasize Empathy and Emotional Intelligence:

Authenticity in the workplace is not just about being honest, it's also about being empathetic. When you are in tune with your emotions and those of others, you can navigate professional relationships with authenticity while maintaining professionalism. Practicing emotional intelligence means being aware of how your disclosures affect others and tailoring your communication accordingly.

- **Example**: If a coworker is going through a tough time, showing empathy without prying into their personal life can help maintain professionalism. Offering support by saying, "I understand this must be difficult, and I'm here if you need anything," shows genuine concern without asking for details that may cross a personal boundary.

e. Present Your True Self Within Professional Expectations:

While authenticity is crucial, it's important to align your authentic self with the expectations of the workplace. This doesn't mean being fake, but rather adapting your communication style to fit the professional environment while staying true to your values and character.

- **Example**: If you're naturally laid-back but work in a formal environment, you can maintain your authenticity by being approachable and personable without compromising professionalism. You might say, "I value a collaborative approach, and I'm here to support you in whatever way is most helpful," instead of using overly casual language.

Authenticity is a powerful tool for building trust and connections, but it requires a balance of openness and discretion. By being mindful of what you share, setting boundaries, and adapting your communication to the context, you can be genuine without oversharing. In professional settings, this balance is especially important, allowing you to maintain your integrity and professionalism while still fostering meaningful relationships.

The Benefits of Vulnerability and Honesty

Vulnerability and honesty are often misunderstood as signs of weakness, but in reality, they are essential elements for building strong, meaningful relationships. When expressed with intention and authenticity, vulnerability allows you to deepen trust, foster understanding, and create a genuine connection with others. Here, we explore how vulnerability and honesty strengthen relationships, provide real-life examples of their impact, and highlight why these qualities are, in fact, sources of strength rather than weakness.

1. How Vulnerability Strengthens Relationships by Deepening Trust and Understanding

At its core, vulnerability is about being open and honest with your emotions and experiences, even when it feels uncomfortable. It requires you to let go of the desire to appear perfect and instead embrace the reality of who you are—your strengths, weaknesses, fears, and challenges. This act of sharing personal truths can significantly deepen trust and understanding in relationships, whether personal or professional.

a. Building Trust Through Authenticity:

When you allow yourself to be vulnerable with someone, you send a powerful message: that you trust them with your true self. In turn, this encourages the other person to reciprocate, creating a cycle of trust that strengthens your connection. Trust is the foundation of any meaningful relationship, and vulnerability accelerates its growth.

- **Example**: Imagine a leader in a company admitting to their team that they don't have all the answers to a particular challenge. By doing so, the leader shows they are human and fosters an environment where team members feel safe to express their own concerns and ideas. This honesty cultivates trust and motivates the team to work collaboratively toward a solution.

b. Fostering Empathy and Understanding:

Vulnerability allows others to see the depth of your emotions and experiences, which in turn fosters empathy. When someone shares a personal struggle or story, it creates an opportunity for the listener to understand their perspective on a deeper level. This shared understanding can bridge gaps in relationships, allowing for more compassion, patience, and connection.

- **Example**: A coworker who shares their experience of balancing work with personal challenges, such as caring for a sick relative, can foster empathy among their peers. Others may begin to appreciate the unique challenges that person faces, leading to greater support, understanding, and collaboration within the team.

c. Deepening Emotional Bonds:

Vulnerability encourages emotional intimacy, especially in personal relationships. When people open up about their insecurities, dreams, or struggles, they form emotional bonds with others who may relate or offer support. This deep connection builds the kind of trust that makes relationships resilient over time.

- **Example**: In a close friendship, one person confiding about their fears or mistakes can lead the other to offer comfort and support. This exchange not only strengthens the relationship but also creates a safe space for mutual openness and understanding, fostering long-term emotional closeness.

2. Examples of How Sharing Personal Challenges or Experiences Can Build Rapport and Influence

Sharing personal experiences and challenges in the right context can build rapport, humanize interactions, and even enhance your influence. Vulnerability is particularly impactful in leadership and mentorship, where being relatable and empathetic is essential for fostering loyalty, respect, and connection.

a. Leaders Who Share Their Struggles Gain Loyalty:

In leadership, vulnerability doesn't undermine authority—it enhances it. Leaders who openly acknowledge their challenges, setbacks, or failures demonstrate that they are approachable, relatable, and human. This kind of vulnerability can inspire loyalty and motivate others by showing that mistakes are a natural part of growth.

· **Example**: A CEO who admits they once struggled with imposter syndrome can inspire employees to feel more comfortable sharing their own challenges. This creates a culture of openness and transparency where employees feel safe to ask for help and admit their own areas of weakness, ultimately improving team morale and performance.

b. Mentors Who Are Honest About Their Journeys Build Trust:

Mentors who are vulnerable with their mentees about the obstacles they've faced on their career journeys build trust and rapport. Sharing stories of failure or self-doubt can make a mentor appear more relatable and approachable, encouraging the mentee to engage more deeply in the relationship.

· **Example**: A mentor in a career development program might share a story about how they were once passed over for a promotion, but how that experience fueled their growth and eventually led them to a better opportunity. This kind of vulnerability can motivate the mentee to view setbacks as learning opportunities and strengthen the mentor-mentee relationship.

c. Personal Stories Foster Connection in Negotiations:

In professional negotiations, vulnerability can create a sense of shared humanity that facilitates compromise. When both parties are willing to share personal motivations or challenges, they are more likely to find common ground, build trust, and create solutions that benefit both sides.

· **Example**: During a business negotiation, one party might share how a certain outcome would affect their company's employees or long-term goals. This kind of transparency can lead the other party to view the situation more holistically, encouraging collaboration instead of competition.

3. Why Vulnerability Is Not a Weakness But a Strength in Fostering Connection and Influence

Vulnerability is often seen as a weakness because it involves exposing aspects of ourselves that we may feel insecure about—such as our emotions, mistakes, or imperfections. However, far from being a liability, vulnerability is a strength that fosters connection and influence. It demonstrates courage, self-awareness, and the willingness to embrace one's authentic self. When expressed appropriately, vulnerability creates meaningful bonds and solidifies trust in relationships.

a. Vulnerability Takes Courage:

It takes courage to let down your guard and reveal your true self to others, especially in a culture that often values strength and stoicism over emotional openness. But the very act of being vulnerable is a powerful display of self-confidence and inner strength. It shows that you're secure enough in yourself to not be defined by your mistakes or insecurities.

- **Example**: In a team meeting, an employee might admit they need help with a particular task, even though asking for help might feel vulnerable. This takes courage but also signals a willingness to collaborate and learn, which ultimately benefits the team and enhances their standing in the workplace.

b. Vulnerability Leads to Influence Through Authenticity:

People are drawn to those who are authentic. When you show vulnerability, you signal that you're real and relatable, which fosters trust. This trust enhances your influence, as people are more likely to follow and be inspired by those they perceive as genuine. By being open about your struggles or emotions, you create a space for others to be vulnerable as well, which builds a foundation for mutual understanding and cooperation.

- **Example**: A manager who admits they made a mistake in a project may initially feel vulnerable but gains respect from their team by showing accountability and honesty. The manager's transparency strengthens their credibility and influence, as the team sees them as both a competent leader and a relatable individual.

c. Vulnerability Enhances Emotional Intelligence:

Being vulnerable requires emotional intelligence—the ability to understand and manage your own emotions, as well as the emotions of others. By being honest about your feelings, you practice self-awareness, empathy, and emotional regulation. These are all key components of emotional intelligence, which is critical for both personal and professional success.

- **Example**: In a personal relationship, being vulnerable about your emotions—such as expressing that you feel hurt or misunderstood—can help resolve conflicts in a constructive way. Instead of bottling up feelings or acting defensively, vulnerability encourages open communication and emotional growth, which strengthens the relationship.

d. Vulnerability Creates a Safe Space for Others:

When you are vulnerable, you create a safe space for others to do the same. This fosters a sense of psychological safety, where people feel comfortable expressing themselves without fear of judgment. In this environment, creativity, collaboration, and deeper connections thrive.

- **Example**: In a brainstorming session, a leader who shares that they're unsure of the best direction for a project invites others to contribute their ideas more freely. By admitting uncertainty, the leader makes it clear that all ideas are welcome, which encourages team members to speak up and contribute without fear of being wrong.

Vulnerability and honesty are powerful tools for building trust, fostering empathy, and enhancing influence. Far from being a weakness, vulnerability is a sign of strength that invites connection and understanding. Whether in personal or professional settings, sharing personal experiences and emotions can deepen relationships, foster collaboration, and create an environment where people feel comfortable being their true selves. By embracing vulnerability, you not only strengthen your own emotional resilience but also pave the way for authentic, meaningful interactions with others.

RESOLVING CONFLICTS – TURNING DISAGREEMENTS INTO O

Approaching Conflicts in a Constructive Manner

Conflict is a natural part of any relationship, whether personal or professional. However, the way we approach conflict can make all the difference in its outcome. When handled constructively, disagreements can become opportunities for growth, deeper understanding, and improved relationships. This section explores techniques for staying calm, focused, and solution-oriented during conflicts, how to depersonalize disagreements, and strategies for avoiding defensiveness while maintaining a respectful tone.

1. Techniques for Staying Calm, Focused, and Solution-Oriented During Conflicts

The ability to stay calm and focused during a disagreement is critical for resolving conflicts in a constructive manner. When emotions run high, it's easy for conflicts to escalate, leading to misunderstandings, frustration, or even damaged relationships. By maintaining composure, you create the space needed for clear thinking, effective communication, and problem-solving.

a. Pause and Breathe:

When conflict arises, it's natural for stress levels to spike, leading to an emotional reaction. To stay calm, pause before responding. Taking a few deep breaths can help regulate your emotions and prevent knee-jerk reactions that could exacerbate the situation. A calm mind allows for better decision-making and helps to keep the conversation productive.

- **Example**: During a heated discussion at work, rather than reacting immediately to a colleague's criticism, take a moment to collect your thoughts. This brief pause can prevent you from saying something in the heat of the moment that you might later regret and allows you to approach the issue with a level-headed response.

b. Stay Focused on the Issue at Hand:

In the midst of conflict, it's easy to get sidetracked by emotions, past grievances, or unrelated issues. Staying focused on the current disagreement helps keep the conversation solution-oriented. Concentrate on the specific problem and avoid bringing up unrelated matters that could derail the discussion or intensify the conflict.

- **Example**: In a disagreement with a friend about a specific event, avoid referencing past conflicts that are unrelated to the current situation. Instead, focus on resolving the immediate issue, which helps prevent the conflict from escalating.

c. Keep the End Goal in Mind:

When engaging in conflict, it's important to remember the ultimate goal: resolution. By keeping the focus on finding a mutually beneficial solution, you shift the conversation from confrontation to collaboration. This mindset helps reduce tension and encourages both parties to work together to resolve the issue.

- **Example**: During a negotiation between two business partners, both may disagree on how to allocate resources for a project. Instead of focusing on their differences, they can shift the conversation toward their shared goal of success for the project, making it easier to find common ground.

2. How to Depersonalize Disagreements and Focus on Problem-Solving

One of the most effective ways to handle conflict is to depersonalize it. When conflicts become personal, emotions can take over, making it difficult to resolve issues objectively. By separating the issue from the person, you can focus on solving the problem without attacking or alienating the other person involved.

a. Avoid Personal Attacks:

Personal attacks or insults only serve to escalate conflict and create resentment. Instead of blaming or criticizing the other person, focus on the issue at hand. Use neutral language that addresses the problem rather than the individual.

- **Example**: Instead of saying, "You always mess things up," try framing the issue as, "We seem to have different approaches to handling this task. Let's discuss how we can improve the process."

b. Use "I" Statements Instead of "You" Statements:

Using "I" statements can help depersonalize the conflict by focusing on your own feelings and needs rather than accusing the other person. This approach prevents the other person from feeling attacked and allows for a more productive conversation.

- **Example**: Instead of saying, "You never listen to me," try saying, "I feel frustrated when I don't feel heard during our conversations. Can we work on improving our communication?"

c. Reframe the Conflict as a Shared Problem:

Rather than viewing the conflict as a battle between you and the other person, reframe it as a shared problem that both parties need to solve together. This shift in perspective promotes collaboration and reduces defensiveness.

- **Example**: In a workplace disagreement over resource allocation, both parties could say, "We have a challenge here in making sure resources are distributed fairly. How can we work together to find a solution that benefits everyone?"

3. Strategies for Avoiding Defensiveness and Maintaining a Respectful Tone

Defensiveness can quickly turn a minor disagreement into a major conflict. When people feel attacked or criticized, they often respond by defending themselves, which can lead to further escalation. By consciously avoiding defensiveness and maintaining a respectful tone, you can create a more productive and respectful dialogue.

a. Listen Actively Without Interrupting:

When someone is expressing their perspective during a conflict, it's easy to jump in with your own point of view, especially if you feel misunderstood or unfairly criticized. However, interrupting or dismissing the other person's concerns can fuel defensiveness and shut down constructive communication. Instead, practice active listening, which involves giving the other person your full attention and acknowledging their point of view.

- **Example**: In a disagreement with a colleague, listen fully to their perspective without planning your response while they speak. After they finish, acknowledge their feelings by saying something like, "I hear that you're frustrated with how things have been handled, and I want to understand your concerns better."

b. Acknowledge the Other Person's Feelings:

Acknowledging the other person's emotions doesn't mean you agree with their point of view, but it shows that you respect and understand how they feel. This simple gesture can go a long way in defusing tension and creating a more open dialogue.

- **Example**: If a friend is upset because they feel neglected, acknowledging their feelings with a statement like, "I understand that you're feeling hurt because we haven't spent much time together," can show empathy and reduce defensiveness, making it easier to move forward in the conversation.

c. Stay Open to Feedback and Criticism:

Defensiveness often arises when we feel attacked or criticized. To avoid this, approach feedback with an open mind. Instead of immediately jumping to defend yourself, consider whether there's any truth to the feedback and how you might use it to grow or improve.

- **Example**: If a coworker gives you constructive criticism about your performance on a project, instead of responding with, "I did my best, and it's not my fault," try saying, "Thank you for the feedback. I'll take that into consideration and see how I can improve next time."

d. Maintain a Calm and Respectful Tone:

Tone of voice plays a significant role in how conflicts unfold. A calm, respectful tone signals that you are open to discussion and willing to find a solution. On the other hand, a raised voice or aggressive tone can escalate the situation, even if your words are neutral. By consciously maintaining a calm tone, you help to keep the conversation productive and respectful.

- **Example**: If you feel yourself becoming frustrated during an argument, take a moment to calm down before continuing the conversation. Lowering your voice and speaking slowly can help prevent the situation from escalating and keep the focus on finding a resolution.

e. Take Responsibility When Necessary:

In any conflict, there's often some level of shared responsibility. Acknowledging your own role in the disagreement can help de-escalate the situation and show the other person that you're willing to take accountability. This can encourage them to do the same and lead to a quicker resolution.

- **Example**: In a disagreement with a partner, you might say, "I realize that I haven't communicated clearly about what I need, and I understand how that has contributed to the misunderstanding."

4. The Power of Emotional Regulation in Conflict Resolution

Managing your emotions during a conflict is crucial to ensuring the conversation remains productive. Emotional regulation involves recognizing when you're feeling overwhelmed and taking steps to manage those feelings before they affect your behavior. By staying emotionally grounded, you're better equipped to resolve the conflict in a positive and constructive way.

a. Recognize Your Triggers:

We all have emotional triggers—certain words, behaviors, or situations that cause us to react more strongly than others. By identifying these triggers, you can become more aware of your emotional responses and take steps to manage them in the moment.

- **Example**: If you know that being interrupted during a conversation is a trigger for you, recognize when it happens and choose to address it calmly, rather than reacting angrily. You might say, "I'd appreciate it if I could finish my point before we move on to another idea."

b. Use Positive Self-Talk:

When emotions run high, it's easy to fall into negative thinking patterns that can fuel defensiveness or frustration. Practicing positive self-talk—reminding yourself that you can handle the situation calmly and constructively—can help shift your mindset and keep you focused on resolution.

- **Example**: If you find yourself feeling defensive in a conflict, remind yourself, "I can listen without taking this personally," or "I'm capable of resolving this issue calmly and respectfully."

Approaching conflicts constructively requires emotional intelligence, communication skills, and a focus on problem-solving. By staying calm, depersonalizing disagreements, and avoiding defensiveness, you can turn conflicts into opportunities for growth, collaboration, and stronger relationships.

De-Escalating Tense Situations

Conflict and tension are inevitable in personal and professional interactions. When emotions run high, disagreements can quickly spiral out of control, leading to damaged relationships or unproductive outcomes. However, de-escalating tense situations is a skill that, when mastered, allows you to navigate conflict with grace, maintain healthy relationships, and find mutually beneficial solutions. This section outlines techniques for diffusing tension, the role of active listening, empathy, and compromise in resolving disputes, and methods for managing emotions and staying composed during challenging conversations.

1. Techniques for Diffusing Tension and Preventing Conflicts from Escalating

When tension arises, the goal is to manage the situation before it intensifies. Proactively applying de-escalation strategies can help keep disagreements from becoming unmanageable, fostering an environment where issues are resolved constructively.

a. Stay Calm and Control Your Tone:

Your tone of voice plays a significant role in de-escalating a situation. Speaking in a calm, steady, and soft tone sends a signal that you're not a threat and encourages the other person to mirror your behavior. Elevated voices and sharp tones, on the other hand, tend to escalate tensions and make the other party feel defensive.

- **Example**: If a colleague is upset during a meeting, resist the urge to match their emotional intensity. Respond in a measured tone with phrases like, "I understand this is frustrating, let's take a moment to talk this through calmly."

b. Acknowledge the Other Person's Emotions:

When someone feels that their emotions are being dismissed or ignored, they may become more frustrated, which can escalate the situation. By acknowledging the other person's feelings, you demonstrate empathy and validate their experience, which can help diffuse the tension.

- **Example**: In a disagreement with a friend, acknowledging their emotions with statements like, "I can see that you're really upset about this," can show that you understand their feelings, making them more likely to calm down and engage in constructive dialogue.

c. Give Space and Time if Needed:

Sometimes, emotions are too heightened to resolve a conflict immediately. In such cases, it's helpful to give the other person (or yourself) space to cool down. Walking away from the conversation for a short period allows both parties to collect their thoughts and return with a clearer perspective.

- **Example**: In the middle of an intense argument, suggesting a short break with a statement like, "Let's take a few minutes to calm down and come back to this," can prevent the situation from escalating further and give both parties time to reflect.

d. Maintain Open Body Language:

Non-verbal communication is just as important as verbal cues when it comes to de-escalating a tense situation. Avoid closed-off body language, such as crossing your arms or looking away.

Instead, maintain eye contact, use open gestures, and keep a relaxed posture, signaling that you're approachable and willing to engage calmly.

- **Example**: If a customer is angry during a service interaction, standing tall with uncrossed arms and maintaining eye contact while nodding can demonstrate that you're listening and open to finding a solution.

e. Use Humility and Apologize When Necessary:

Humility can be disarming in tense situations. Admitting your mistakes or apologizing for any misunderstandings can quickly reduce the intensity of an argument. It shows that you're not interested in winning the argument, but in finding a resolution.

- **Example**: In a disagreement with a partner, saying, "I realize I may have misunderstood your point earlier, and I apologize for that," can lower the other person's defensiveness and open the door for more constructive communication.

2. The Importance of Active Listening, Empathy, and Compromise in Resolving Disputes

Resolving disputes is not about "winning" but about understanding the other party's perspective, empathizing with their emotions, and finding a solution that satisfies both sides. Active listening, empathy, and compromise are key elements in this process.

a. Active Listening:

Active listening involves giving the speaker your full attention, reflecting on their words, and showing that you're engaged in the conversation. It's not just about hearing what the other person says, but about understanding their message, both verbally and non-verbally.

- **Techniques**:
    - **Paraphrasing**: Repeat back what the other person has said in your own words to confirm understanding. For example, "So, if I understand correctly, you feel that I haven't been clear in my communication?"
    - **Nodding and Eye Contact**: These non-verbal cues show that you're engaged in the conversation and actively processing what's being said.
    - **Asking Open-Ended Questions**: Encourage the other person to explain their perspective in more detail by asking questions like, "Can you tell me more about what you're feeling?"

Active listening reduces tension by making the other person feel heard and understood, which is often enough to diffuse a conflict.

b. Empathy:

Empathy involves putting yourself in the other person's shoes and attempting to understand their emotional state and perspective. Demonstrating empathy shows that you care about how the other person feels, which can create an atmosphere of collaboration rather than confrontation.

- **Example**: In a workplace disagreement, empathizing with a colleague's frustration by saying, "I can see how the current workload must be overwhelming for you," helps to build rapport and shifts the focus from blame to problem-solving.

Empathy also plays a critical role in finding compromises, as it allows you to see the conflict from multiple angles and consider solutions that benefit all parties involved.

c. Compromise:

In any conflict, both parties usually need to make concessions to reach a resolution. Compromise involves finding a middle ground where both sides feel their needs are at least partially met. This doesn't mean you have to sacrifice your core values, but rather, it's about being flexible and open to alternatives.

- **Example**: During a conflict about project deadlines, you might offer to adjust the timeline slightly while still ensuring key milestones are met. This shows a willingness to accommodate the other person's needs while maintaining your priorities.

Compromise reduces friction by fostering a spirit of cooperation and mutual respect, allowing both sides to feel that they've contributed to the solution.

3. How to Manage Emotions and Stay Composed in Challenging Conversations

Managing your own emotions during a tense conversation is crucial for preventing conflicts from escalating. Emotional intelligence, self-regulation, and mindfulness can help you stay composed and respond thoughtfully, even when the situation is stressful or uncomfortable.

a. Recognize Your Emotional Triggers:

We all have emotional triggers that make us more likely to react impulsively. Whether it's being interrupted, criticized, or dismissed, recognizing what triggers your emotional responses allows you to pause and choose how to react rather than letting emotions take control.

- **Example**: If being interrupted is a trigger for you, acknowledge the emotion but choose to respond calmly by saying, "I'd like to finish my point before we move on."

b. Use Mindfulness to Stay Present:

Mindfulness involves staying present in the moment, rather than getting lost in past grievances or future anxieties. By focusing on the here and now, you can manage emotions more effectively and prevent yourself from reacting based on assumptions or preconceived notions.

- **Techniques**:
    - **Deep Breathing**: When you feel your emotions rising, take a few deep breaths to calm your mind and body.
    - **Body Scanning**: Pay attention to physical sensations of tension in your body, such as tightness in your chest or shoulders. Consciously relax those areas to reduce stress.
    - **Reframing Thoughts**: Shift your focus from negative thoughts to more constructive ones. For exam-

ple, instead of thinking, "They're attacking me," try reframing it as, "They're upset, and I need to understand why."

c. Set Boundaries to Protect Your Emotions:

During especially challenging conversations, it's important to set boundaries to protect your emotional well-being. This may involve calmly stating that you need to take a break from the discussion or politely declining to engage in unproductive arguments.

- **Example**: If a conversation is becoming too heated, say, "I think we both need some time to cool off. Can we revisit this conversation in an hour?"

d. Practice Self-Compassion:

It's easy to become critical of yourself when conflicts don't go as planned, but practicing self-compassion allows you to stay grounded and resilient. Recognize that everyone makes mistakes, and give yourself permission to learn and grow from each interaction.

- **Example**: After a difficult conversation, rather than dwelling on what you could have done differently, remind yourself, "I did my best, and I can use this experience to improve my conflict resolution skills."

De-escalating tense situations requires emotional awareness, effective communication, and a willingness to find common ground. By applying techniques such as active listening, empathy, and compromise, and managing your own emotions, you can prevent conflicts from escalating and create an environment where problems are solved constructively.

Turning Disagreements into Opportunities for Growth

Conflicts and disagreements, while often uncomfortable, are an inevitable part of relationships—whether personal or professional. When approached with the right mindset, they can serve as catalysts for growth, improved communication, and deeper understanding. Rather than seeing conflict as something to avoid or fear, it can be viewed as an opportunity to learn, grow, and build stronger, more resilient relationships. In this section, we will explore how conflicts can lead to personal and professional growth, strategies for turning disagreements into learning experiences, and real-life examples of how constructive conflict resolution can foster long-term trust and respect.

1. How Conflicts Can Lead to Deeper Understanding, Improved Communication, and Stronger Relationships

At its core, conflict often arises from differing perspectives, needs, or expectations. When conflicts are handled constructively, they can lead to valuable insights into yourself and others, allowing for more meaningful connections.

a. Conflict Encourages Honest Communication:

In many cases, conflict brings underlying issues to the surface. When people are in conflict, they're more likely to voice their true thoughts and feelings, which may have been previously suppressed. This can lead to more honest and open communication, as both parties are compelled to express themselves clearly.

- **Example**: A manager and an employee might have ongoing friction about workload expectations. During a conflict, the employee may finally express that they feel overwhelmed, leading to a discussion about time management, delegation, and prioritization. This honest conversation can resolve misunderstandings and create an environment where both parties feel heard.

b. Understanding Different Perspectives:

When you engage in constructive conflict, it provides a window into the other person's worldview, priorities, and values. By listening and understanding their perspective, you gain a deeper understanding of their needs and motivations, which can foster empathy and respect.

- **Example**: In a disagreement between friends, one friend may feel that the other isn't putting enough effort into the relationship. This disagreement provides an opportunity for both to share their perspectives—one may realize they've been neglecting the friendship due to external pressures, while the other may gain insight into why they feel undervalued. This new understanding can strengthen the bond between them.

c. Strengthening Relationships Through Resolution:

When conflicts are resolved in a healthy manner, relationships often emerge stronger than before. The process of working through a disagreement builds trust and demonstrates that both parties are committed to finding a solution rather than walking away. The ability to navigate challenges together strengthens the relationship's foundation.

- **Example**: A couple that successfully works through a major disagreement, such as differing career priorities, may come out of the conflict with a greater appreciation for each other's values and a deeper sense of partnership. Knowing that they can resolve issues together builds long-term resilience in their relationship.

2. Strategies for Using Disagreements as Learning Experiences to Grow Personally and Professionally

To turn conflicts into opportunities for growth, it's essential to approach them with the right mindset. Rather than focusing on "winning" or proving the other person wrong, adopt a mindset of learning and improvement. The following strategies can help you use disagreements as a pathway for personal and professional development.

a. Shift Your Mindset to View Conflict as an Opportunity:

Instead of viewing conflict as a negative event, reframe it as a chance to gain new insights. Recognize that disagreements can be productive if handled with an open mind and a willingness to learn. This mindset shift allows you to embrace conflict as part of the growth process.

- **Example**: If a colleague disagrees with your approach to a project, rather than feeling defensive, view it as an opportunity to learn from their perspective. You might discover a more efficient method or gain insight into areas you hadn't considered.

b. Focus on the Issue, Not the Person:

It's easy to take disagreements personally, but productive conflict resolution requires separating the issue from the individual. Focus on addressing the problem at hand without assigning blame or letting emotions cloud the discussion. This depersonalized approach allows for a more objective and constructive resolution.

- **Example**: If a family member disagrees with how you handled a situation, instead of seeing it as a personal attack, try to understand their concerns about the situation itself. This will keep the conversation focused on finding a solution, rather than creating tension between individuals.

c. Embrace Feedback and Self-Reflection:

Conflicts often provide valuable feedback about your behavior, communication style, or assumptions. Use disagreements as opportunities for self-reflection. Consider how your actions or words may have contributed to the conflict and how you can grow from the experience.

- **Example**: After a heated discussion with a team member, reflect on whether your tone or choice of words could have been misinterpreted or caused unnecessary tension. This self-reflection can help you communicate more effectively in the future.

d. Practice Active Listening and Empathy:

One of the most important skills in turning conflict into a learning experience is active listening. By truly listening to the other person's perspective, rather than planning your rebuttal, you gain insights that can inform your own growth. Coupled with empathy, this approach allows you to see the conflict from their point of view, fostering understanding and collaboration.

- **Example**: In a disagreement with a partner, practice listening without interrupting. After they've spoken, reflect back what you heard to show you understand. This not only helps you learn more about their perspective but also deepens your emotional connection.

e. Seek Win-Win Solutions:

Growth-oriented conflict resolution focuses on finding solutions that benefit both parties. A win-win approach fosters collaboration rather than competition, encouraging both sides to work together toward a mutually beneficial outcome.

- **Example**: If you and a colleague disagree on a project timeline, seek a compromise that accommodates both of your needs. Perhaps adjusting the timeline slightly allows the project to maintain quality while reducing stress for both parties.

3. Examples of How Constructive Conflict Resolution Can Build Long-Term Trust and Respect

When conflicts are resolved in a constructive and respectful manner, they often lead to stronger relationships, enhanced trust, and long-term mutual respect. Below are examples of how addressing disagreements can lead to positive outcomes.

a. Workplace Conflict Resolution Leads to Greater Team Cohesion:

In a corporate setting, a project team may experience tension due to differing opinions about the project's direction. Rather than allowing the disagreement to fester, the team leader facilitates an open discussion where all viewpoints are heard. Through active listening and compromise, the team agrees on a new approach that incorporates everyone's input. By resolving the conflict constructively, the team builds stronger trust and becomes more cohesive, improving their ability to collaborate on future projects.

> • **Key Takeaway**: Constructive conflict resolution fosters an environment of respect and collaboration, allowing teams to work more effectively together.

b. Personal Disagreement Strengthens a Friendship:

Two long-time friends have a falling out over a misunderstanding regarding a planned vacation. One friend feels hurt because they believed the other canceled the trip without consulting them. Instead of letting the resentment grow, they sit down and discuss the situation openly. Both friends share their feelings and clarify their intentions. The conversation leads to a deeper understanding of each other's communication styles and expectations, ultimately strengthening their bond.

> • **Key Takeaway**: Resolving personal conflicts through open dialogue can enhance trust and deepen emotional connections in friendships.

c. Family Conflict Turns into a Learning Opportunity:

A family disagreement arises when a parent and their adult child clash over lifestyle choices. Rather than escalating into a heated argument, they decide to engage in a calm conversation where both sides explain their perspectives. The parent gains insight into the child's reasoning, and the child understands the parent's concerns. This respectful exchange not only resolves the immediate conflict but also improves their long-term relationship by building mutual respect.

- **Key Takeaway**: Family conflicts, when handled with empathy and open communication, can lead to greater understanding and lasting respect.

d. Business Partnership Conflict Yields Innovation:

In a business partnership, two co-founders disagree about the future direction of their company. Instead of avoiding the conflict, they engage in a productive conversation where each presents their vision. Through respectful debate, they uncover new ideas that neither had considered before, leading to an innovative solution that propels the company forward. The conflict, rather than tearing the partnership apart, becomes a catalyst for growth and success.

- **Key Takeaway**: Conflicts in business partnerships can lead to innovative solutions when both parties are committed to resolving disagreements constructively.

Conflicts, when approached with the right mindset and strategies, offer valuable opportunities for growth, learning, and strengthening relationships. By embracing conflict as a natural part of life, focusing on understanding and problem-solving, and practicing active listening and empathy, you can turn disagreements into opportunities for deeper connections, enhanced communication, and mutual respect. Whether in personal relationships, professional settings, or family dynamics, constructive conflict resolution builds long-term trust and fosters growth.

NETWORKING LIKE A PRO – EXPANDING YOUR CIRCLE OF I

Networking is often seen as one of the most powerful tools for personal and professional growth. Building a strong network goes beyond simply collecting business cards or adding connections on social media—it's about forming meaningful, mutually beneficial relationships. In this chapter, we'll explore effective networking strategies for social and professional contexts, the importance of prioritizing quality over quantity, how to make a lasting impression when meeting new people, and techniques for cultivating deeper, authentic connections.

Effective Networking Strategies in Social and Professional Contexts

Networking is valuable in a variety of settings, from casual social gatherings to formal business events. While the context may change, the principles of effective networking remain consistent.

Building a strong network requires a strategic approach, where authenticity, mutual respect, and shared interests are central to the relationship.

a. Understanding Your Purpose for Networking:

Before attending any event or engaging with others, it's important to clarify your purpose for networking. Are you looking to expand your professional network, find potential collaborators, or simply meet new people who share common interests? Understanding your goals helps you approach networking with intentionality, allowing you to connect with individuals who can support your personal and professional growth.

- **Example**: If you're attending a professional conference, your goal might be to meet industry leaders or potential clients. This intention will guide how you engage with others and help you focus on making connections that align with your objectives.

b. Being Prepared with a Personal Introduction:

One of the most important aspects of networking is being able to introduce yourself confidently. Whether in a social or professional setting, having a clear and concise introduction helps others understand who you are and what you're passionate about. Your introduction should highlight your name, profession or interests, and what drives you.

- **Example**: "Hi, I'm Sarah, and I work in digital marketing. I specialize in helping businesses grow their online presence through social media strategy and content marketing. I'm passionate about learning new trends in the industry and always looking to connect with like-minded professionals."

c. Listening More Than You Speak:

While networking involves sharing information about yourself, the most effective networkers are those who listen attentively. Asking thoughtful questions and showing genuine interest in others' stories or experiences can leave a lasting impression. By listening more than you speak, you demonstrate that you value the other person's perspective, which helps establish trust and rapport.

- **Example**: At a networking event, instead of focusing on talking about your own achievements, ask the person you're speaking with about their projects or career journey. Listen actively, and follow up with relevant questions that show you're engaged in the conversation.

d. Following Up and Staying Connected:

Networking doesn't end after the initial conversation. To build meaningful relationships, it's important to follow up with the people you meet. This can be as simple as sending a personalized email or message, referencing something you discussed during your conversation. Staying in touch regularly, whether through social media or occasional check-ins, helps maintain the connection and keeps the relationship alive.

- **Example**: After attending a conference, you could send a follow-up email to someone you connected with, saying, "It was great meeting you at the marketing summit! I really enjoyed our conversation about social media trends. Let's keep in touch and explore ways we might collaborate in the future."

2. The Importance of Quality Over Quantity in Building Your Network

While it may be tempting to collect as many contacts as possible, a large network isn't necessarily a valuable one. When it comes to networking, quality far outweighs quantity. Building a few meaningful, strong relationships is much more impactful than having a long list of superficial contacts.

a. Prioritizing Meaningful Connections:

In both social and professional settings, focus on developing relationships with people who share common values, interests, or goals. Networking isn't about how many people you know, but how well you know them. Cultivating deeper connections with a smaller group allows for stronger trust and mutual support, which leads to more fulfilling and productive relationships.

- **Example**: Instead of trying to meet everyone at a large networking event, focus on having a few in-depth conversations with people who align with your professional interests. These meaningful connections are more likely to lead to collaborations or long-term relationships.

b. Nurturing Existing Relationships:

A successful networker doesn't just focus on meeting new people; they also invest time in maintaining and nurturing existing relationships. Staying connected with the people you already know ensures that your network remains active and engaged.

Regularly checking in with colleagues, friends, and mentors, even if just to offer support or share an update, strengthens your bond over time.

- **Example**: Send occasional messages to former colleagues or classmates, asking about their current projects or offering congratulations on their achievements. These small gestures help keep your relationship strong, making it easier to collaborate or support each other in the future.

3. How to Make a Lasting Impression When Meeting New People

First impressions are crucial in networking. Making a positive and memorable impression can open doors for future opportunities, both personally and professionally. While networking can sometimes feel intimidating, focusing on key elements such as authenticity, confidence, and active listening can help you stand out and create lasting relationships.

a. Projecting Confidence Without Being Overbearing:

Confidence is an essential trait when making a first impression. However, there's a fine line between confidence and arrogance. When meeting new people, it's important to project confidence in your abilities and who you are without coming across as overbearing. Confidence can be shown through positive body language, clear communication, and maintaining eye contact.

- **Example**: When introducing yourself at a networking event, stand tall, offer a firm handshake, and speak clearly.

This demonstrates that you're confident in who you are, but also open and approachable.

b. Showing Genuine Interest:

People are more likely to remember you if you show genuine interest in them. Ask thoughtful questions, listen actively, and engage with their stories. By being present in the conversation and expressing curiosity, you demonstrate that you value the other person, which leaves a lasting impression.

- **Example**: If someone shares a challenge they're facing in their work, ask follow-up questions that show you're invested in the conversation. "That sounds like a difficult situation—how have you been approaching it so far?" This kind of response shows empathy and engagement.

c. Sharing Value Without Bragging:

While it's important to share what you bring to the table, no one likes a braggart. Focus on sharing value in a way that feels collaborative rather than boastful. Highlight your strengths or expertise in the context of how you can support others, rather than focusing solely on your own achievements.

- **Example**: Instead of saying, "I'm the best at managing social media campaigns," you could say, "I've had great success with social media strategies in the past, and I'd love to explore how we could work together on something similar."

4. Techniques for Cultivating Meaningful Connections Rather Than Superficial Contacts

Building a network of meaningful connections takes time, effort, and authenticity. Rather than focusing on creating as many connections as possible, prioritize building relationships based on trust, mutual respect, and shared goals. Below are some techniques to help you develop deep and lasting connections.

a. Be Authentic and Transparent:

People are drawn to authenticity. When you're genuine in your interactions, others are more likely to trust you and feel comfortable building a relationship. Avoid trying to impress others by pretending to be someone you're not; instead, let your true self shine through in your conversations.

- **Example**: If you're unsure about a topic being discussed, don't be afraid to admit it. "I'm not very familiar with that area—could you tell me more?" This honesty shows humility and a willingness to learn, which can strengthen your connection with others.

b. Offer Help and Support:

A strong network is built on mutual support. One of the best ways to deepen your relationships is by offering help or resources without expecting anything in return. Whether it's connecting someone with a colleague, offering advice, or sharing helpful information, giving to others strengthens the bond between you.

- **Example**: If a new connection mentions they're looking for job opportunities in a particular field, offer to introduce them to someone in your network who works in that industry. This small gesture can leave a lasting impression and lead to a deeper connection.

c. Be Consistent in Your Interactions:

Consistency is key when it comes to building meaningful relationships. Follow up after your initial meeting and stay in touch regularly. Whether it's through periodic check-ins, sharing relevant content, or scheduling catch-ups, consistent communication shows that you're invested in the relationship.

- **Example**: After meeting someone at a networking event, send them an article related to a topic you discussed. "I came across this article about marketing trends and thought of our conversation at the event—hope you find it helpful!"

Networking effectively is not about collecting business cards or growing your social media follower count; it's about building genuine, meaningful relationships that contribute to both personal and professional growth. By prioritizing quality over quantity, making lasting impressions, and cultivating connections based on trust, authenticity, and mutual support, you can expand your circle of influence and create a network that truly supports your long-term goals. Whether you're attending social gatherings, business events, or simply connecting with others in your everyday life, these strategies will help you network like a pro.

Maintaining and Nurturing Relationships Over Time

Building a network is just the first step in expanding your circle of influence; maintaining and nurturing those relationships over time is equally, if not more, important. Relationships, whether personal or professional, require consistent attention and care to stay strong and productive. In this section, we'll explore why follow-up is crucial to keeping relationships alive, strategies for staying in touch without appearing needy or intrusive, and how to balance networking with building deep, long-lasting connections.

1. Why Follow-Up is Key to Keeping Relationships Alive

Meeting someone for the first time is a great start, but the real value of networking lies in the follow-up. Consistent, thoughtful follow-up turns one-time encounters into ongoing relationships. Without it, even the most promising connections can fizzle out. Following up demonstrates that you're serious about maintaining the relationship and that you value the person you've connected with.

a. Building Trust and Consistency:

Consistent follow-up is a powerful way to build trust. When you stay in touch with someone after the initial meeting, you show that you're dependable and genuinely interested in fostering the relationship. Trust is at the core of all strong relationships, and one of the best ways to develop it is through ongoing, meaningful communication.

- **Example**: After meeting a new connection at a business event, send a thoughtful email within a day or two, mentioning something specific from your conversation. This demonstrates that you were fully present and engaged during your interaction and helps establish a solid foundation for future communication.

b. Keeping the Relationship Active:

Relationships, especially professional ones, can easily fade away without consistent communication. If you don't make an effort to follow up, it's likely that both parties will forget the initial interaction. Staying in touch ensures that the relationship remains active and that you stay on each other's radar for potential future collaborations or opportunities.

- **Example**: You meet a potential business partner at a conference, and a few weeks later, you come across an article related to their work. Sending the article with a brief note, "This reminded me of our conversation at the conference—thought you'd find it interesting," keeps the relationship alive without being overly formal.

c. Creating Opportunities for Collaboration:

Follow-up is also a way to explore potential opportunities for collaboration. Many successful partnerships, business deals, or creative projects begin with a simple follow-up after a chance meeting. By reaching out regularly, you open the door for future collaborations or opportunities that may not have been apparent during your initial encounter.

- **Example**: After a meeting, reach out to your new contact a few weeks later with an idea for a project or collaboration. "I've been thinking about our conversation at the networking event and had an idea I'd love to discuss with you—would you be open to a quick call?"

2. Strategies for Staying in Touch Without Appearing Needy or Intrusive

While follow-up is important, it's equally essential to strike the right balance in your communication. Reaching out too often or in a way that feels forced can come across as needy or intrusive, which can damage the relationship instead of nurturing it. Here are some strategies to maintain contact while ensuring your communication feels natural and welcome.

a. Timing Your Follow-Ups Appropriately:

The timing of your follow-ups matters. Immediately after an initial meeting, a prompt message within a day or two is ideal. However, after that, you don't need to reach out too frequently. The goal is to maintain regular, yet spaced-out communication that feels natural rather than overwhelming.

- **Example**: After your initial follow-up, give some time—two to three weeks—before reaching out again. You can then continue with quarterly check-ins, sharing relevant articles, updates, or invitations to events.

b. Offering Value in Each Interaction:

Each time you reach out, aim to offer something of value rather than just asking for a favor or checking in without purpose. Offering value can be as simple as sharing an interesting article, connecting your contact with someone in your network, or offering insights related to their work. By providing value, your communication becomes a positive interaction rather than a request.

- **Example**: If you see an industry report or news piece that aligns with their interests, send it with a note like, "This report made me think of the challenges you mentioned last time we spoke—I hope it's helpful."

c. Respecting Boundaries and Being Mindful of Their Time:

While it's important to stay in touch, it's equally essential to respect the other person's time and boundaries. Don't overwhelm them with excessive messages or requests, and always make it clear that you respect their schedule. For instance, if you're asking for a meeting, provide flexible options and be mindful of their commitments.

- **Example**: Instead of sending several messages in a short span of time, you can say something like, "I know you're busy, so no rush on this—I just wanted to share this when you have a moment to review it."

d. Using Multiple Communication Channels:

To avoid being overly formal or repetitive, mix up the ways you communicate. Use a combination of emails, social media, phone calls, and even in-person meetings when appropriate. This approach keeps things dynamic and prevents your interactions from feeling too rigid or transactional.

- **Example**: After sending a couple of follow-up emails, switch things up by interacting with their posts on LinkedIn or sending a quick message via social media.

3. Balancing Networking with Building Deep, Long-Lasting Connections

Networking can sometimes feel like a numbers game, but true success comes from building deep, long-lasting connections rather than superficial relationships. Here's how you can balance your efforts in expanding your network while also nurturing the meaningful relationships you've already established.

a. Investing Time in Key Relationships:

Not every connection requires the same level of attention. Identify the relationships that matter most—whether for professional development, collaboration, or personal support—and prioritize investing time and effort in those connections. Building deep relationships with a select few will ultimately bring more value than trying to maintain shallow relationships with many.

- **Example**: If you've developed a strong connection with a mentor or key business partner, invest more time in those relationships by scheduling regular catch-ups, sharing insights, or seeking their advice on significant matters.

b. Being Authentic in Your Interactions:

Authenticity is the foundation of any strong, long-lasting relationship. Whether you're networking with someone new or maintaining an existing relationship, always aim to be genuine in your interactions. People can easily sense when communication is insincere or transactional. By showing genuine interest and concern, you create deeper, more lasting bonds.

- **Example**: Instead of always focusing on what the other person can offer you, approach conversations with a mindset of mutual benefit. Ask how you can help or support them in their goals, rather than always focusing on your own agenda.

c. Balancing New Connections with Existing Ones:

As you continue to network and meet new people, don't neglect your existing relationships. Make time for both meeting new contacts and nurturing long-standing connections. While expanding your network is important, it's the quality of your relationships that will lead to long-term success.

- **Example**: If you've recently met a new contact at a networking event, follow up and stay in touch, but don't forget to check in with an old mentor or colleague as well. Scheduling time for both ensures that all your relationships remain strong.

d. Being Patient and Letting Relationships Develop Naturally:

Building deep connections takes time. Don't rush the process or expect immediate results from networking. Allow relationships to evolve naturally through consistent communication and shared experiences. Over time, these relationships will become stronger and more valuable.

- **Example**: Instead of expecting an immediate business deal or opportunity after meeting someone, focus on cultivating the relationship over several months. Over time, the connection may lead to collaborations or partnerships in a more organic and natural way.

Maintaining and nurturing relationships over time is the key to building a strong, influential network. By following up with purpose, offering value in your interactions, respecting boundaries, and balancing new connections with deepening existing ones, you can cultivate long-lasting relationships that will support your personal and professional growth. The strength of your network doesn't lie in the number of people you know, but in the depth and quality of the relationships you've nurtured over time.

Building a Support System Through Meaningful Connections

Building a strong support system is essential for personal and professional success. Meaningful connections not only provide encouragement and motivation but also offer guidance, opportunities, and emotional support. A well-developed network can inspire you, help you overcome challenges, and create pathways to success. This section will explore how to surround yourself with people who inspire, motivate, and support you, the techniques for creating reciprocal relationships, and the long-term value of having a robust and diverse network.

1. How to Surround Yourself with People Who Inspire, Motivate, and Support You

The people you surround yourself with can have a profound impact on your mindset, attitude, and achievements. If you're intentional about building relationships with individuals who inspire, motivate, and support you, you'll find yourself more empowered to pursue your goals and navigate obstacles.

a. Identifying Key Qualities in Your Support Network:

The first step in surrounding yourself with the right people is identifying the qualities that align with your values, ambitions, and emotional needs. Look for individuals who not only share your vision but also challenge you to grow. These may include mentors, colleagues, friends, or family members who provide encouragement, honest feedback, and accountability.

- **Example**: Consider people who exhibit resilience, optimism, and integrity—individuals who stay positive during difficult times and offer constructive advice when you need guidance.

b. Seeking Out Mentors and Role Models:

Mentorship is an invaluable component of a strong support system. Mentors offer wisdom, perspective, and expertise that can help guide you in your personal and professional journey. Role models, even if you don't have a personal connection with them, can inspire you through their achievements and approaches to life.

- **Example**: If you admire someone in your industry, don't hesitate to reach out to them for advice or mentorship. Attend industry events or networking opportunities where you can meet potential mentors who can guide you in your career.

c. Cultivating Relationships with Positive and Motivated Individuals:

Energy is contagious, and when you spend time with positive, motivated individuals, you're likely to adopt those traits yourself.

Seek out people who not only have an optimistic outlook on life but who also take action to achieve their goals. Surrounding yourself with proactive, driven individuals will keep you focused and energized in your own pursuits.

- **Example**: Join groups, communities, or clubs where members are passionate about personal development, professional growth, or shared interests. Engaging in environments where positivity and motivation are the norm can significantly elevate your mindset.

2. Techniques for Creating Reciprocal Relationships That Benefit Both Parties

In order to build a strong, supportive network, it's important to foster reciprocal relationships—those that are mutually beneficial. True connections are built on mutual trust, respect, and the desire to see one another succeed. By investing in others and offering value, you create relationships that benefit both parties in the long term.

a. Offering Value Before Asking for Help:

Reciprocity is the foundation of any meaningful relationship. When you focus on giving first—whether it's by offering advice, sharing resources, or providing support—you build goodwill. In turn, when you need help or guidance, your network will be more likely to offer support because they know you've already contributed to the relationship.

- **Example**: If you're building a professional relationship, offer to help with a project, provide a useful introduction, or share relevant insights before seeking advice or assistance.

b. Finding Common Ground and Shared Interests:

Building reciprocal relationships starts with finding common ground. People are more likely to support one another when there's a shared interest, goal, or value. When you connect on a deeper level—whether it's through a shared passion or common experience—it becomes easier to offer and receive support.

- **Example**: If you're meeting a new contact at a networking event, try to discover shared interests or challenges. This could be anything from a mutual professional goal to a passion for a specific cause. A shared connection creates a solid foundation for future interactions.

c. Being Consistent and Reliable:

Reciprocal relationships require ongoing effort and attention. Being reliable and consistent in your communication and actions reinforces the trust that you've established. When people know they can count on you, they are more likely to reciprocate with the same level of commitment.

- **Example**: If a colleague or friend asks for advice, follow through promptly and thoughtfully. Show up when it matters—whether it's offering encouragement during difficult times or celebrating successes together.

d. Fostering Open Communication:

Healthy relationships thrive on open communication. Expressing your needs, boundaries, and goals allows for a more transparent and respectful dynamic. When both parties clearly communicate their expectations and desires, it's easier to create a mutually supportive relationship.

- **Example**: If you're working on a collaborative project, have an open conversation about how you can best support each other's goals and contributions. This ensures that both parties feel valued and heard.

3. The Long-Term Value of Having a Robust and Diverse Network

A strong, diverse network is one of the most valuable assets you can cultivate. Over time, it provides not only professional opportunities but also emotional support and personal growth. A diverse support system allows you to gain new perspectives, challenge your thinking, and access resources that can enrich your life in countless ways.

a. Diversity of Perspectives and Ideas:

When you surround yourself with a diverse group of people, you expose yourself to a wide range of perspectives and ideas. This diversity fuels creativity, innovation, and problem-solving. A network that includes individuals from different backgrounds, industries, and experiences will offer insights you may not have considered on your own.

- **Example**: If you're facing a challenge at work, seeking advice from someone in a different industry may provide a fresh perspective that helps you see the problem in a new light.

b. Increased Opportunities for Collaboration and Growth:

A robust network opens the door to countless opportunities. The more diverse and extensive your network, the more likely you are to encounter potential collaborators, mentors, or business opportunities. Additionally, these relationships can lead to personal growth as you learn from others' experiences and challenges.

- **Example**: Networking at industry events, social gatherings, or community organizations can lead to new business ventures, joint projects, or mentorship opportunities that would have otherwise been inaccessible.

c. Emotional and Professional Support in Challenging Times:

Life and work are full of ups and downs, and having a support system in place during challenging times can make all the difference. A strong network of friends, colleagues, and mentors can provide encouragement, advice, and resources when you're facing difficult situations. Knowing you have people who believe in you helps build resilience.

- **Example**: When navigating a career transition or personal challenge, having a network of supportive people—whether they offer emotional support or professional advice—can help you stay motivated and confident.

d. Expanding Influence and Visibility:

As your network grows, so does your influence. A robust network gives you access to a wider audience, whether you're trying to promote a project, start a business, or advocate for a cause. The people in your network can amplify your message, refer you to others, and provide opportunities for increased visibility.

- **Example**: A strong online presence coupled with a diverse network can lead to invitations to speak at events, collaborate on projects, or contribute to high-profile initiatives, all of which expand your reach and influence.

Building a support system through meaningful connections is essential for personal and professional success. By surrounding yourself with individuals who inspire and motivate you, fostering reciprocal relationships, and cultivating a diverse and robust network, you can create a foundation for long-term growth, resilience, and success. The true value of a strong network lies not in the number of contacts but in the depth and quality of the connections you've nurtured over time.

BUILDING INFLUENCE AT WORK – WINNING COLLEAGUES AN

The Importance of Social Skills in the Workplace

In today's work environment, technical knowledge and expertise are only part of what makes a person successful. Equally important are strong social skills, often referred to as "soft skills" or "interpersonal skills." These skills, including the ability to communicate effectively, collaborate with others, and navigate social dynamics, are essential for building influence in the workplace. Whether you're leading a team, working alongside colleagues, or managing relationships with clients, strong interpersonal skills are the key to fostering collaboration, mutual respect, and long-term success.

How Strong Interpersonal Skills Are Linked to Career Success, Leadership, and Workplace Harmony

Social skills are often what set great leaders apart from those who struggle to gain influence in the workplace. These skills include everything from active listening and clear communication to empathy and conflict resolution. While technical expertise is critical for performing your job, the ability to connect with others on a personal level is what makes a lasting impact. Studies have shown that employees with strong interpersonal skills are more likely to be promoted, build strong networks, and create a positive work environment.

a. Career Advancement and Leadership:

Individuals who excel in building strong relationships with their colleagues, superiors, and clients often find it easier to move up the career ladder. Interpersonal skills such as emotional intelligence, communication, and conflict resolution are highly valued by employers because they contribute to team cohesion and organizational success. These individuals are often seen as leaders, even if they don't hold formal leadership roles, because they can navigate complex social dynamics and inspire trust in others.

- **Example**: A manager who can effectively motivate their team and handle conflicts diplomatically is likely to gain the respect of their colleagues, which can lead to more opportunities for career advancement.

b. Workplace Harmony and Collaboration:

Social skills also play a crucial role in creating a harmonious work environment. Employees who can build positive relationships with their colleagues and supervisors are more likely to contribute to a collaborative and respectful workplace. This, in turn, leads to greater job satisfaction, higher productivity, and lower turnover rates. Interpersonal skills help you understand different perspectives, resolve misunderstandings, and foster an atmosphere where everyone feels valued.

- **Example**: A colleague who regularly checks in with team members and offers support when needed will likely be seen as a valuable asset, promoting a culture of collaboration and mutual respect.

c. Client Relationships and Business Success:

In client-facing roles, strong social skills are indispensable. Whether you're negotiating contracts, managing client expectations, or addressing concerns, the ability to connect with clients on a personal level builds trust and loyalty. Clients who feel understood and respected are more likely to continue doing business with you and refer you to others.

- **Example**: A client manager who can empathize with a client's concerns and provide solutions tailored to their needs is more likely to build a long-term, successful partnership.

Techniques for Building Relationships with Colleagues and Clients That Foster Collaboration and Respect

Building strong relationships at work doesn't happen overnight. It requires consistent effort, empathy, and communication. Whether you're working with colleagues on a daily basis or interacting with clients occasionally, the following techniques can help you foster collaboration, mutual respect, and influence in your workplace relationships.

a. Active Listening and Empathy:

Active listening is one of the most critical components of strong interpersonal relationships. When you listen actively, you're not just hearing the words someone says—you're also paying attention to their tone, body language, and emotional state. Empathy, the ability to understand and share the feelings of others, goes hand-in-hand with active listening. When colleagues or clients feel heard and understood, they're more likely to trust and respect you.

- **Example**: During a team meeting, instead of interrupting or waiting for your turn to speak, listen carefully to your colleague's point, acknowledge their perspective, and build on it in a way that demonstrates you've understood their concerns.

b. Clear and Transparent Communication:

Good communication is essential for building strong relationships in the workplace. This means being clear and concise in your messages, whether you're discussing a project, providing feedback, or addressing concerns. Transparent communication fosters trust because it shows that you're honest, open, and willing to engage in meaningful dialogue.

- **Example**: When providing feedback to a colleague, be specific and direct, focusing on the issue rather than making vague or overly critical statements. Offer suggestions for improvement and be open to receiving feedback yourself.

c. Collaboration and Teamwork:

Being a good team player is one of the best ways to build influence in the workplace. When you're willing to collaborate, share credit for successes, and support others in achieving their goals, you demonstrate that you're invested in the success of the entire team, not just your own. This willingness to collaborate fosters mutual respect and strengthens your professional relationships.

- **Example**: If a project requires input from multiple departments, take the initiative to reach out to colleagues, coordinate efforts, and ensure that everyone is aligned. This not only helps the project run smoothly but also shows that you value teamwork.

d. Consistency and Reliability:

Building strong relationships with colleagues and clients also requires consistency and reliability. People need to know they can count on you to follow through on your commitments and deliver high-quality work. By being dependable, you build a reputation for trustworthiness, which is essential for long-term success.

- **Example**: If you promise a colleague or client that you'll deliver a report by a specific deadline, make sure to follow through. If unforeseen circumstances arise, communicate promptly and offer an alternative solution.

The Role of Social Intelligence in Navigating Office Politics and Team Dynamics

Social intelligence, the ability to understand and manage complex social relationships, is a vital skill for navigating office politics and team dynamics. It involves being aware of the emotions, motivations, and power dynamics at play in your workplace and using that knowledge to build strong, positive relationships. Understanding office politics doesn't mean engaging in manipulative behavior; rather, it means being mindful of how decisions are made, how relationships are formed, and how influence is built.

a. Understanding Power Dynamics:

Every workplace has its own set of power dynamics, whether formal or informal. Social intelligence allows you to recognize these dynamics and navigate them effectively. This means being aware of who holds decision-making authority, who influences key decisions, and how to position yourself in a way that aligns with your goals while maintaining integrity.

- **Example**: If you're working on a project and know that a particular department head has significant influence over its approval, take the time to build a relationship with that person, understand their priorities, and align your project's goals with theirs.

b. Reading and Responding to Emotional Cues:

Part of social intelligence is being able to read the emotional cues of others—whether it's a colleague who's frustrated or a client who's hesitant about a proposal. By being attuned to these cues, you can respond in a way that addresses their concerns and builds trust. This not only improves your relationships but also helps you avoid misunderstandings or conflicts.

- **Example**: If a colleague seems unusually quiet during a meeting, don't ignore the behavior. Instead, check in with them afterward to see if they have concerns that weren't voiced. This shows that you're attentive to their emotions and open to addressing any issues.

c. Building Alliances Without Alienating Others:

In workplaces where office politics are prevalent, it's essential to build alliances and form relationships that can help you achieve your goals. However, it's equally important to do so without alienating others. Building alliances should not come at the expense of burning bridges with colleagues or undermining others' efforts. Instead, focus on creating win-win situations where both parties benefit.

- **Example**: If you're collaborating with a particular team or department, make an effort to build relationships across the organization, rather than focusing all your attention on one group. This ensures that you maintain positive relationships throughout the workplace.

d. Adapting to Team Dynamics:

Every team has its own unique dynamics, shaped by the personalities, working styles, and preferences of its members. Social intelligence involves adapting to these dynamics while maintaining your authenticity. Being flexible in your communication style and approach can help you work more effectively with different team members, whether they're detail-oriented planners or big-picture thinkers.

- **Example**: If you're leading a team of individuals with different working styles, consider adjusting your leadership approach to accommodate their preferences. For example, you might provide more structure and detailed guidance for team members who prefer clear direction while allowing more creative freedom for those who thrive on autonomy.

Strong social skills are essential for building influence in the workplace, fostering collaboration, and achieving long-term success. By developing interpersonal skills such as active listening, clear communication, and social intelligence, you can navigate complex team dynamics, build trust with colleagues and clients, and advance your career. The ability to connect with others on a personal level, understand social dynamics, and respond with empathy and integrity will help you build a positive reputation and lasting professional relationships.

Gaining the Respect and Admiration of Colleagues

Earning the respect and admiration of your colleagues is essential for building a positive work environment and advancing your career. It's not just about demonstrating your technical expertise or completing tasks on time, but about embodying the qualities that make you a reliable, empathetic, and collaborative team member. Respect is cultivated through consistent actions, professional integrity, and an ability to connect with others in a meaningful way. Admiration, on the other hand, comes from going beyond expectations, leading by example, and showing humility in your accomplishments.

How to Earn Respect Through Reliability, Professionalism, and Empathy

Respect in the workplace is built on the foundation of reliability, professionalism, and empathy. These qualities show your colleagues that you are dependable, considerate of others, and committed to the shared success of the team.

a. Reliability:

Reliability is one of the most fundamental qualities in earning respect. When your colleagues know they can count on you to deliver quality work on time, follow through on commitments, and contribute consistently, they are more likely to trust and respect you. Reliability also means being accountable for your actions and taking responsibility when things go wrong.

- **Example**: If you commit to completing a project by a specific deadline, ensure that you meet or exceed that expectation. If unforeseen circumstances arise, communicate proactively and offer solutions, such as asking for an extension or adjusting the scope of the project.

b. Professionalism:

Professionalism is about conducting yourself with integrity, respect, and courtesy in all interactions. This includes maintaining a positive attitude, treating others with respect regardless of their role or status, and adhering to the ethical standards of your workplace. Professionalism is also about staying composed under pressure and handling difficult situations with grace and tact.

- **Example**: When faced with a challenging client or an internal disagreement, avoid reacting impulsively. Instead, take the time to assess the situation, consider the perspectives of others involved, and respond in a calm and respectful manner.

c. Empathy:

Empathy involves understanding and valuing the emotions, perspectives, and experiences of your colleagues. By showing genuine concern for their well-being and demonstrating compassion in your interactions, you can build stronger, more respectful relationships. Empathy also involves being flexible and adaptable, recognizing when someone may need support, and offering it without judgment.

> · **Example**: If a colleague is overwhelmed with a tight deadline or personal challenges, offering to assist with their workload or simply listening to their concerns can make a significant difference in building respect and trust.

Strategies for Leading by Example and Inspiring Confidence in Your Abilities

Leadership is not solely defined by a title or position; it is demonstrated through actions, behavior, and the way you influence others. By leading by example, you inspire confidence in your abilities and encourage others to follow your lead. People are more likely to respect and admire you when they see that you uphold high standards for yourself and treat others with respect and kindness.

a. Setting High Standards:

Leading by example means holding yourself to high standards in your work, communication, and conduct. When you consistently strive for excellence, others will notice your dedication and be inspired to follow suit. This includes being diligent, organized, and proactive in your tasks, as well as maintaining a positive work ethic even in challenging situations.

- **Example**: If your team is working on a tight deadline, show your commitment by putting in extra effort, staying organized, and helping others stay on track. Your work ethic will inspire those around you to give their best as well.

b. Maintaining a Positive Attitude:

Your attitude and approach to challenges significantly influence how others perceive you. By maintaining a positive, solution-oriented mindset, even in the face of adversity, you can instill confidence in your team. When you focus on finding solutions rather than dwelling on problems, you encourage others to adopt the same perspective.

- **Example**: If a project hits a major roadblock, instead of expressing frustration or assigning blame, approach the situation with a calm and constructive attitude. Lead a discussion focused on identifying solutions and moving forward.

c. Inspiring Confidence Through Competence and Consistency:

Competence and consistency are essential for inspiring confidence. When colleagues see that you are knowledgeable, skilled, and capable of handling challenges, they will trust your judgment and abilities. Consistency means showing up as your best self every day, maintaining high-quality work, and responding predictably in a professional manner.

- **Example**: If you consistently deliver excellent results and handle difficult situations with composure, your colleagues will view you as someone they can rely on, both in times of success and difficulty.

The Role of Humility, Collaboration, and Inclusivity in Gaining Admiration and Influence

While competence and leadership are critical, they must be balanced with humility, collaboration, and inclusivity to gain the genuine admiration of your colleagues. People are more likely to admire and be influenced by those who show humility in their achievements, foster collaboration, and ensure that everyone feels included and valued.

a. Humility in Achievements:

Humility means recognizing that success is often a team effort and being willing to share credit with others. It involves staying grounded and not letting personal achievements inflate your ego. Colleagues are more likely to admire someone who is confident in their abilities but remains humble, acknowledging the contributions of others.

- **Example**: After successfully completing a major project, instead of seeking personal praise, make a point to highlight the contributions of your team members. Recognize their hard work and express gratitude for their efforts.

b. Fostering Collaboration:

Great leaders and colleagues are those who actively promote collaboration and encourage everyone to contribute their strengths. By creating a culture of teamwork, you show that you value diverse perspectives and believe in collective success. Collaboration also involves being open to feedback, learning from others, and recognizing that no one person has all the answers.

- **Example**: In meetings or group projects, make an effort to invite input from quieter team members or those who may not always speak up. By doing so, you demonstrate that you value everyone's opinions and contributions.

c. Practicing Inclusivity:

Inclusivity is about ensuring that everyone feels welcome, valued, and respected in the workplace. This means being mindful of diversity in all its forms—whether it's gender, ethnicity, background, or experience—and creating an environment where all voices are heard. Inclusive practices not only build admiration and respect but also lead to a more creative and innovative team.

- **Example**: When forming teams for a new project, make an effort to include individuals from different departments or backgrounds, encouraging a diverse exchange of ideas. In doing so, you show that you value a wide range of perspectives and are committed to inclusivity.

Earning the respect and admiration of your colleagues requires a balanced combination of reliability, professionalism, empathy, and humility. By leading by example, fostering collaboration, and embracing inclusivity, you can inspire confidence in your abilities and build influence in the workplace. The path to admiration is not about seeking recognition or asserting dominance but about consistently demonstrating your value as a team player, leader, and respectful colleague. Through your actions, you can create a work environment where trust, respect, and admiration thrive.

Influencing Team Dynamics and Fostering a Positive Work Environment

In any workplace, team dynamics play a crucial role in determining both individual and collective success. The ability to positively influence these dynamics is key to fostering a collaborative, supportive, and productive environment. Leaders and team members alike can shape the culture and environment by using strategies that promote harmony, trust, and mutual respect. When individuals are engaged and feel valued, the team becomes more cohesive, creative, and motivated to reach common goals.

Techniques for Positively Influencing Group Dynamics and Creating a Collaborative, Supportive Workplace

Group dynamics are the unseen forces that influence how individuals within a team interact, communicate, and work together. These dynamics can either propel a team toward success or contribute to dysfunction. To ensure that your team operates in a healthy, collaborative way, it's essential to actively nurture these dynamics with intentional techniques.

a. Encouraging Open Communication:

Open and honest communication is the cornerstone of a positive work environment. When team members feel they can express their ideas, concerns, and opinions freely, it leads to greater innovation and problem-solving. Encouraging an environment where everyone's voice is heard ensures that the team feels valued and fosters a sense of belonging.

- **Example**: Start team meetings with an open discussion where everyone has an opportunity to contribute. Create a safe space where all input is respected and considered, even if it challenges existing ideas.

b. Promoting Inclusivity and Collaboration:

Inclusivity is essential to group dynamics because it ensures that all members of the team feel involved and appreciated. Collaboration thrives when individuals with different strengths and perspectives work together toward a common goal. By fostering an inclusive environment, you promote teamwork and shared ownership of outcomes.

- **Example**: Assign tasks that require cross-departmental collaboration or pair team members with complementary skill sets. Encourage diverse perspectives and make inclusivity a priority in decision-making processes.

c. Setting Clear Roles and Expectations:

Unclear roles and expectations can lead to confusion, conflict, and frustration within a team. To foster positive group dynamics, make sure that each team member understands their role, responsibilities, and how they contribute to the team's overall success. When everyone knows what is expected of them, it reduces tension and enables smoother collaboration.

- **Example**: At the start of a project, outline each person's role and responsibilities in a project plan. Regularly check in to ensure everyone is aligned with the expectations and progress is on track.

d. Encouraging Mutual Support:

A supportive team is one in which individuals feel comfortable offering help and accepting it from others. Encouraging mutual support means creating a culture where collaboration and team-work are prioritized over competition. When team members know that they can rely on each other, it strengthens trust and fosters a positive, cohesive environment.

- **Example**: Recognize and reward instances where team members go out of their way to support each other, whether through collaboration on a challenging task or offering assistance to a colleague in need.

e. Celebrating Wins and Acknowledging Contributions:

Celebrating successes and acknowledging the contributions of each team member fosters positivity and boosts morale. It helps to reinforce the value that individuals bring to the team, motivating them to continue giving their best efforts. Recognizing accomplishments, both big and small, can create a more engaged and driven team.

- **Example**: At the end of a project, hold a team celebration where you highlight the contributions of different members and reflect on the success of the team as a whole. Expressing gratitude and acknowledging effort fosters continued enthusiasm and loyalty.

The Importance of Emotional Intelligence in Managing Conflicts, Motivating Teams, and Building Consensus

Emotional intelligence (EQ) is the ability to understand and manage both your own emotions and the emotions of others. High EQ is essential for navigating team dynamics, as it helps in managing conflicts, motivating teams, and building consensus. Leaders with emotional intelligence are better equipped to foster a harmonious work environment, where issues are addressed constructively, and team members feel motivated and supported.

a. Managing Conflicts with Emotional Intelligence:

Conflicts are inevitable in any team setting, but how they are managed can significantly impact team dynamics. Emotional intelligence enables you to approach conflicts with empathy and self-awareness, de-escalating situations before they spiral out of control. Instead of reacting impulsively, emotionally intelligent individuals seek to understand the root causes of the conflict and focus on finding solutions that benefit everyone involved.

- **Example**: If two team members are disagreeing on a project approach, instead of taking sides, a leader with emotional intelligence would facilitate a conversation where both parties can share their perspectives. By validating each person's concerns and looking for common ground, the conflict can be resolved in a way that strengthens the team.

b. Motivating Teams through Understanding Individual Needs:

Each team member is motivated by different factors—some may be driven by personal achievement, while others find motivation in collaboration and teamwork. Emotional intelligence allows you to recognize these individual differences and tailor your approach accordingly. By understanding what drives each person, you can create a more motivating and supportive work environment.

- **Example**: When leading a team, take time to understand what motivates each member. Offer public recognition to those who appreciate being acknowledged in front of others, while providing private, meaningful feedback to those who prefer a more personal approach.

c. Building Consensus through Empathy and Active Listening:

In a team setting, building consensus is often necessary to move forward on projects and initiatives. Emotional intelligence plays a crucial role in this process, as it allows you to listen actively, empathize with differing viewpoints, and guide the team toward a mutually agreeable solution. Rather than pushing your own agenda, focus on understanding the perspectives of others and fostering collaborative decision-making.

- **Example**: When your team is divided on a course of action, take the time to listen to each person's viewpoint and demonstrate empathy for their concerns. Facilitate a discussion that prioritizes shared goals and encourages compromise, leading to a decision that everyone can support.

How to Foster an Environment of Mutual Respect, Trust, and Open Communication

Creating a workplace environment built on mutual respect, trust, and open communication is essential for positive team dynamics. When individuals feel respected and trusted, they are more likely to engage in meaningful collaboration, share their ideas, and contribute to the team's overall success. Establishing these values requires intentional actions and consistent reinforcement.

a. Modeling Respectful Behavior:

Respect starts from the top. As a leader or influential team member, it's important to model respectful behavior in every interaction. This means actively listening to others, valuing their contributions, and treating everyone—regardless of their role or background—with dignity. When you consistently demonstrate respect, it sets a standard for the entire team.

- **Example**: In meetings, make a point to listen actively to each team member, avoid interrupting, and show genuine interest in their ideas. This demonstrates that you respect their input and value their contributions.

b. Building Trust Through Transparency and Accountability:

Trust is built over time through transparency, honesty, and accountability. To foster trust within your team, be open about your decisions, share relevant information, and take responsibility for your actions. When team members see that you are trustworthy, they are more likely to reciprocate, leading to a culture of mutual trust.

- **Example**: If a project faces setbacks or challenges, be transparent with your team about the situation. Instead of placing blame or hiding information, discuss the obstacles openly and work together to find solutions.

c. Encouraging Open Communication and Feedback:

Open communication is essential for building strong team dynamics. It involves creating an environment where individuals feel comfortable sharing their ideas, providing feedback, and discussing challenges without fear of judgment. Encouraging open communication helps to prevent misunderstandings and fosters a culture of continuous improvement.

- **Example**: Regularly solicit feedback from your team, both formally and informally. Encourage an open-door policy where individuals feel comfortable discussing any concerns or suggestions they have.

Positively influencing team dynamics and creating a supportive work environment requires intentional actions, emotional intelligence, and a commitment to fostering mutual respect and trust. By promoting open communication, collaboration, and inclusivity, you can shape a workplace culture where individuals feel valued and motivated to contribute to the team's success. When these dynamics are in place, conflicts are managed constructively, teams are motivated, and the overall work environment becomes a place of growth, innovation, and shared accomplishment.

SUSTAINING RELATIONSHIPS – THE LONG-TERM APPROACH

Maintaining Friendships and Connections Over Time

Relationships, whether personal or professional, are essential to a fulfilling life, but they require ongoing effort to remain strong and healthy. In today's fast-paced world, it's easy to lose touch with people, even those we care about deeply. However, maintaining meaningful relationships is possible with the right strategies, dedication, and intention. Sustaining long-term connections requires regular communication, showing appreciation, and balancing the ebb and flow of life's demands.

Why Relationships Require Ongoing Effort to Remain Strong and Healthy

The foundation of any lasting relationship is built on mutual trust, respect, and shared experiences. While the initial spark of a friendship or connection may come naturally, keeping the relationship strong over time takes conscious effort. People change, and circumstances evolve, which can challenge the strength of the bond. It's important to nurture relationships consistently, even when life becomes hectic.

a. Consistency is Key:

One of the most important factors in maintaining a strong relationship is consistency. Whether it's through regular check-ins or finding ways to spend quality time together, consistently showing up for the people in your life builds trust and demonstrates your commitment to the relationship. Consistency doesn't mean being available all the time; rather, it's about maintaining a presence that fosters stability and dependability.

- **Example**: Regularly schedule time for a coffee catch-up with a friend or send a message every few weeks to check in on how they're doing. This consistent effort ensures that the connection remains strong over time.

b. Embracing Change:

People grow, and their priorities shift over time. Friendships and relationships that survive the long haul are often those that adapt to these changes. Being open to how both you and the other person evolve can strengthen the bond by showing that you value the connection no matter what life throws your way.

· **Example**: A friend who used to be available for spontaneous adventures may now be more focused on their career or family. Embracing this shift and finding new ways to connect will allow the friendship to flourish in its new form.

c. Effort vs. Expectation:

It's easy to assume that a relationship will remain strong without consistent effort, but relationships can weaken if one party expects the other to do all the work. Both individuals need to contribute to keep the relationship healthy, especially as time passes. When both people invest in maintaining the connection, the relationship becomes more resilient and fulfilling.

· **Example**: If one friend is always the one initiating conversations or meet-ups, the relationship can feel one-sided. Making an effort to reach out and plan together ensures that both parties feel valued and appreciated.

Techniques for Staying Connected with Friends and Colleagues, Even with Busy Schedules

Life gets busy, and maintaining relationships can become challenging when you're balancing work, personal responsibilities, and other commitments. However, with some creativity and intention, it's possible to stay connected even during hectic times. Small gestures and thoughtful communication go a long way in keeping relationships alive, despite the limitations of time.

a. Leverage Technology:

Technology has made it easier than ever to stay connected with people regardless of physical distance or busy schedules.

From social media to messaging apps, there are numerous ways to stay in touch with friends, family, and colleagues. A quick message, voice note, or even a shared post can remind someone that you're thinking of them, even if you don't have time for a long conversation.

- **Example**: If you're pressed for time, send a quick message or share an article that made you think of the person. It keeps the communication lines open without requiring a lengthy conversation.

b. Make Time for What Matters:

Though life gets busy, prioritizing the people who matter to you is essential. It may not always be possible to spend hours catching up, but setting aside time for meaningful interactions strengthens relationships. Even 10 minutes of focused, intentional conversation can have a big impact.

- **Example**: If you're swamped with work, plan a brief but meaningful call with a friend during your commute or lunch break. Scheduling time ensures that you don't let weeks or months slip by without checking in.

c. Use Small Gestures to Stay Connected:

Not all communication needs to be grand or time-consuming. Sometimes, small gestures are enough to keep a connection alive. These gestures show that you value the relationship and are thinking of the person, even when you're busy.

- **Example**: Sending a quick message on someone's birthday, forwarding a funny meme, or mailing a handwritten note are simple ways to maintain a connection without a large time investment.

d. Balance Quality and Quantity:

Maintaining relationships isn't always about frequent communication but about the quality of your interactions. A single meaningful conversation can carry more weight than several brief check-ins. Focusing on the quality of your time together—whether in person or virtually—helps maintain the strength of your connection, even if you don't talk often.

- **Example**: When you do meet or catch up, focus on being present and engaging in deep conversations. Ask about what matters to them, listen intently, and show empathy for their challenges and successes.

The Importance of Showing Appreciation and Gratitude in Long-Term Relationships

In long-term relationships, whether personal or professional, it's easy to take people for granted as familiarity grows. However, showing appreciation and gratitude regularly is crucial in sustaining the relationship over time. Acknowledging and valuing the contributions of others not only strengthens your bond but also reinforces a culture of kindness and respect.

a. Recognizing Contributions:

People appreciate being recognized for their efforts, whether they've supported you in a tough time or consistently contributed to your life in meaningful ways. Expressing gratitude for what they bring to your life reinforces the relationship and encourages continued mutual support.

- **Example**: If a friend has been a consistent source of advice and support, don't hesitate to let them know how much you value their presence in your life. A simple "thank you for always being there for me" can deepen the bond between you.

b. Practicing Active Gratitude:

Gratitude is more than just a verbal expression—it can also be shown through actions. Practicing active gratitude involves doing things that show the other person how much you care. This might include offering help, giving thoughtful gifts, or simply spending time with the person when they need it.

- **Example**: If you're grateful for a colleague's support on a project, offer to help them with their work or buy them a coffee to express your appreciation. These small gestures demonstrate that you recognize and value their contributions.

c. Celebrating Milestones and Achievements:

Celebrating milestones and achievements, whether personal or professional, shows that you are invested in the other person's life and success. These celebrations don't have to be extravagant—sometimes, just acknowledging a friend's promotion or celebrating an anniversary can go a long way.

- **Example**: If a friend has achieved a significant milestone, like completing a challenging project or reaching a career goal, celebrate their success with a thoughtful message, a congratulatory card, or a small gathering.

d. Gratitude in Professional Relationships:

In professional relationships, showing appreciation is equally important. Recognizing the contributions of colleagues or clients not only fosters positive relationships but also enhances collaboration. Expressing gratitude in the workplace can boost morale, increase engagement, and create a more supportive environment.

· **Example**: After a successful project, take the time to thank your team for their hard work. Acknowledging the contributions of each team member creates a positive, collaborative culture that strengthens long-term professional relationships.

Building Relationships That Stand the Test of Time

Maintaining long-term relationships—whether friendships or professional connections—requires ongoing effort, thoughtful communication, and a commitment to staying connected. Life's demands may create challenges, but prioritizing the people who matter most ensures that those relationships remain strong and rewarding over time. By consistently showing appreciation, adapting to change, and making time for meaningful interactions, you can sustain the relationships that enrich your life. Whether it's a close friend, a colleague, or a long-distance connection, the effort invested in keeping relationships alive will pay off in the form of trust, loyalty, and deeper connections that stand the test of time.

Consistent, Meaningful Interactions

In the fast-paced world we live in, relationships often get neglected as we prioritize work, responsibilities, and other commitments. However, maintaining closeness and trust in relationships requires regular, thoughtful interactions. These consistent efforts, no matter how small, play a pivotal role in sustaining long-term connections and deepening bonds with others. The key to building trust and emotional security in relationships lies in showing up consistently and engaging in meaningful exchanges that reinforce the relationship's importance.

How Regular, Thoughtful Interactions Help to Maintain Closeness and Trust in Relationships

Human connections thrive on regular interaction. When you engage with someone on a regular basis, even through brief conversations or gestures, it signals that the relationship is valued. Over time, these regular touchpoints build emotional security, allowing both parties to feel supported and appreciated.

a. Building Emotional Security:

Consistency creates a sense of reliability, which fosters emotional security in a relationship. When individuals know they can count on each other for support or a simple check-in, it strengthens the bond. Emotional security arises when people feel they can trust that someone will be there for them, whether in times of joy or challenge.

- **Example**: Regularly checking in on a friend or partner—even with a quick message—lets them know you care about their well-being. It doesn't have to be an elaborate conversation; a small, thoughtful act like asking how their day was can create a sense of stability in the relationship.

b. Reinforcing Commitment:

Consistent interactions help reinforce the commitment both parties have to the relationship. Whether it's a friendship, romantic relationship, or professional connection, regularly showing up for the other person conveys that you're invested in maintaining the relationship. This ongoing commitment strengthens the bond and deepens the connection over time.

- **Example**: Scheduling a weekly phone call with a friend or a monthly coffee meeting with a colleague demonstrates that you're committed to the relationship and want to nurture it, despite the demands of a busy life.

c. Avoiding Drift in Relationships:

Inconsistent communication can create emotional distance. Over time, relationships can drift if both parties don't make an effort to stay connected. Even if the relationship was once close, a lack of regular interaction can lead to feelings of neglect or detachment. Regular, meaningful communication keeps the relationship fresh and prevents emotional drift.

- **Example**: A friend who moved away may feel disconnected if you don't stay in touch. Regularly sending updates or planning video chats can prevent the relationship from fading, ensuring that the bond remains strong despite physical distance.

Examples of Small, Meaningful Gestures That Can Make a Big Difference in Sustaining Connections

It's easy to think that maintaining relationships requires grand gestures, but small, thoughtful actions often have the most significant impact. These little acts of kindness or moments of attention demonstrate that you're thinking of the other person and value the connection.

a. Sending Thoughtful Messages:

A simple message like "Thinking of you" or "Hope you're doing well" can make a big difference in sustaining a relationship. These small, unexpected gestures show that you care, even if you don't have time for a longer conversation. Regularly sending brief messages to check in helps maintain closeness, especially in busy or distant relationships.

- **Example**: Sending a quick text to a friend when you see something that reminds you of them—like a funny meme or an article related to their interests—keeps the connection alive without requiring a lot of time.

b. Remembering Important Dates:

Acknowledging important dates such as birthdays, anniversaries, or significant events in someone's life can strengthen the bond between you. These small acts of recognition show that you pay attention to what matters to them, which helps deepen emotional connection.

- **Example**: Remembering a colleague's work anniversary and congratulating them can make them feel valued and appreciated in the workplace. Similarly, wishing a friend happy birthday or acknowledging a significant milestone can have a lasting positive impact.

c. Offering Help or Support:

Offering support during challenging times or even just lending a helping hand with everyday tasks is a powerful way to sustain relationships. Small gestures, like bringing over a meal when someone is busy or offering a ride when they're in need, show that you care and are there for them when it matters most.

- **Example**: If a friend is going through a tough time at work, sending them an encouraging message or offering to help with a task can provide comfort and strengthen the connection.

d. Celebrating Successes:

Celebrating the successes of those in your life, no matter how big or small, fosters positivity in the relationship. Acknowledging their achievements shows that you're invested in their happiness and growth, which builds mutual trust and appreciation.

- **Example**: Congratulating a friend on completing a project or landing a new job, or sending them a card to celebrate a personal milestone, reinforces the relationship by showing you're genuinely happy for their success.

Why Consistency Is Key to Building Trust and Emotional Security in Relationships

Trust is the cornerstone of any meaningful relationship, and consistency plays a critical role in building that trust. When people experience consistent, positive interactions, it reassures them that the relationship is stable and secure. This emotional security allows both parties to feel safe in being vulnerable and open with each other, knowing that the other person will be there to support them.

a. Creating Dependability:

Being consistent in how you interact with others creates dependability. When people know they can count on you to be there, it builds trust. Dependability doesn't mean being available 24/7; rather, it's about consistently showing up in meaningful ways that demonstrate reliability and care.

- **Example**: Always responding to a friend's messages within a reasonable time, or keeping your promises to meet up or offer support, creates a foundation of trust. They'll know that you're someone they can rely on.

b. Reinforcing Positive Expectations:

Consistency also reinforces positive expectations in the relationship. When your interactions are regularly positive and thoughtful, it sets the expectation that future interactions will be equally supportive and meaningful. This creates an environment of emotional security, where both individuals feel safe and valued.

- **Example**: If you consistently offer a listening ear when your friend needs to talk, they'll naturally feel comfortable coming to you in the future when they need support, knowing that you'll be there for them.

c. Building Emotional Intimacy:

Regular, meaningful interactions help build emotional intimacy in a relationship. Whether in friendships, romantic relationships, or professional connections, emotional intimacy deepens as both parties share their thoughts, feelings, and experiences over time. This closeness is strengthened through consistent, thoughtful communication that fosters trust and understanding.

- **Example**: In a romantic relationship, regularly spending quality time together and engaging in open, honest conversations deepens emotional intimacy and creates a strong foundation of trust.

d. Preventing Miscommunication:

Consistency in communication also helps prevent miscommunication and misunderstandings, which can damage trust. When people communicate sporadically, it's easier for misunderstandings to arise, which can lead to unnecessary tension. Regular, clear communication helps clarify expectations and keeps both parties on the same page.

- **Example**: Regularly checking in with a colleague on a shared project helps avoid confusion or misalignment. By keeping communication consistent, you ensure that both of you are aligned and working toward the same goal.

Nurturing Relationships Despite Busy Schedules

Balancing personal and professional commitments with maintaining meaningful relationships can feel like a constant juggling act. In today's fast-paced world, it's easy to get swept up in the demands of work, personal responsibilities, and daily routines, often leaving little time for nurturing connections with loved ones, friends, and colleagues. However, maintaining these relationships is crucial for both personal fulfillment and long-term professional success. Prioritizing meaningful interactions, even when life gets busy, helps preserve the bonds that provide emotional support, shared growth, and collaboration.

How to Balance Personal and Professional Commitments with Maintaining Meaningful Relationships

Achieving balance between your commitments and relationships requires thoughtful planning, flexibility, and a genuine desire to stay connected with the important people in your life. While it may seem challenging, finding ways to nurture relationships amidst a busy schedule is not impossible. It involves making intentional efforts to invest in relationships that matter most.

a. Time Management and Setting Priorities:

Effectively managing your time is key to balancing commitments and relationships. When your schedule is packed with work meetings, deadlines, and personal tasks, it's crucial to evaluate where relationships fit into your priorities. Relationships, like any other important part of life, need time and attention. Scheduling time to connect with loved ones, whether through a simple phone call or a planned get-together, helps keep those relationships strong.

· **Example**: You might decide to set aside specific time each week for personal connections, like a weekend brunch with family or a mid-week coffee break with a friend. By adding these social interactions to your calendar, they become part of your routine rather than an afterthought.

b. Quality Over Quantity:

In a busy life, the quality of your interactions often outweighs the quantity. Meaningful relationships don't necessarily require hours of conversation or frequent meet-ups. Instead, they thrive on genuine, focused interactions. A short but meaningful exchange—where you're fully present—can have a far greater impact than prolonged but distracted communication.

· **Example**: If you have a busy workday, sending a thoughtful message or making a five-minute phone call to check in with a close friend can go a long way in showing that you value the relationship, even if you can't spend much time together.

c. Flexibility and Adaptability:

Flexibility is essential for maintaining relationships amidst the unpredictability of personal and professional life. There will be times when work or family obligations take precedence, and you may not have the time or energy for socializing. In such cases, it's important to be adaptable and communicate openly with those in your life. People generally understand when life gets busy, especially if you've built a foundation of trust and mutual respect.

· **Example**: If a friend or colleague reaches out to make plans but your schedule is packed, suggesting an alternative date or offering a virtual catch-up session shows that you still value the relationship despite current constraints.

Techniques for Prioritizing Important Relationships and Managing Time Effectively

Effectively managing time for relationships involves not only setting priorities but also employing specific strategies that allow you to maintain connection without feeling overwhelmed. A few simple techniques can help ensure that your relationships don't fall by the wayside amidst a hectic schedule.

a. Schedule Regular Check-Ins:

One of the most effective ways to maintain relationships is to schedule regular check-ins. Whether it's a weekly phone call, a monthly dinner, or a quarterly catch-up over coffee, creating a regular routine helps ensure you stay connected with the people who matter most. By intentionally setting aside time for these interactions, you're more likely to follow through, even when your schedule is full.

· **Example**: Schedule a weekly call with a close friend or family member, or set up a recurring monthly lunch with a colleague. The consistency of these check-ins keeps relationships active and strong.

b. Use Technology to Stay Connected:

In today's digital age, technology offers an excellent solution for staying connected with friends, family, and colleagues when time is limited. Video calls, instant messaging, and social media platforms allow for quick, meaningful interactions that can bridge the gap when in-person meetings aren't possible. Even a brief message or a thoughtful comment on a social media post can keep the connection alive.

- **Example**: If you're unable to meet in person, scheduling a virtual coffee break with a friend or sending them a quick message to check in can help you maintain the relationship despite physical distance.

c. Make Relationships a Part of Your Daily Routine:

Instead of viewing relationships as something separate from your daily routine, try to integrate them into your life in a natural way. Small gestures, like sending a message on your commute, sharing a meal, or even catching up while running errands together, can ensure that relationships don't get neglected due to time constraints.

- **Example**: You might call a friend or family member while driving home from work, or invite a colleague to join you for lunch, blending relationship-building into your existing schedule.

d. Delegate and Outsource Where Possible:

One way to free up time for nurturing relationships is to delegate or outsource tasks that don't require your direct attention. Whether it's hiring help for household chores or delegating professional tasks to team members, offloading some of your responsibilities can open up space in your schedule for connecting with others.

- **Example**: By hiring a cleaning service or using meal delivery, you free up personal time that can be spent with loved ones, ensuring that relationships don't take a backseat to everyday tasks.

Why Making Time for Friends, Family, and Colleagues is Essential for Long-Term Personal and Professional Success

Maintaining relationships is more than just a social obligation—it's essential for long-term success in both your personal and professional life. Strong, supportive relationships provide a foundation for emotional well-being, motivation, and collaboration, all of which are critical for achieving success and fulfillment.

a. Emotional Support and Well-Being:

Relationships are a key source of emotional support. Friends, family, and colleagues offer encouragement, help us navigate challenges, and provide a sense of belonging. In the long term, having a strong network of supportive people contributes to better mental health, reduced stress, and increased resilience. Regular social interaction has even been linked to longevity and improved overall well-being.

- **Example**: During a particularly stressful time at work, having close friends or family to talk to can help alleviate the pressure, offering both emotional relief and practical advice.

b. Professional Growth and Collaboration:

In the workplace, relationships play a critical role in career development. Building and maintaining strong professional relationships fosters collaboration, enhances communication, and increases opportunities for growth and success. Colleagues, mentors, and clients are more likely to support you, share opportunities, and collaborate when you've taken the time to nurture the relationship.

- **Example**: Regularly checking in with colleagues and maintaining a good rapport with them can lead to stronger teamwork and increased opportunities for collaboration on important projects.

c. Enhanced Creativity and Problem-Solving:

Surrounding yourself with a diverse network of people allows you to tap into different perspectives and ideas, enhancing creativity and problem-solving. Relationships with a variety of individuals—from friends and family to colleagues and mentors—offer unique insights that can help you think outside the box and approach challenges in new ways.

- **Example**: A discussion with a friend outside of your industry might spark a creative idea for a project you're working on, or feedback from a colleague might help you solve a problem more efficiently.

d. Mutual Benefit and Reciprocity:

Relationships thrive on reciprocity, where both parties benefit from the connection. In the long term, strong relationships offer mutual support, whether in the form of emotional encouragement, professional collaboration, or shared resources. By consistently nurturing your relationships, you create a network of people who are willing to offer help, advice, or opportunities when needed.

- **Example**: A mentor you've maintained a relationship with over the years might offer guidance or open doors to new opportunities when you're facing a career transition.

In conclusion, sustaining relationships over time requires ongoing effort, intentional communication, and thoughtful actions, even when life gets busy. By prioritizing meaningful connections and incorporating regular, consistent interactions, you can maintain trust and closeness with friends, family, and colleagues. Small gestures of appreciation, expressions of gratitude, and conscious time management play a significant role in nurturing these bonds. Ultimately, investing in your relationships—both personal and professional—leads to greater emotional well-being, long-term success, and a robust support system for life's challenges and achievements.

CONCLUSION: A LIFETIME OF FRIENDSHIP AND INFLUENCE

Recap of Key Principles

As we come to the close of this journey through the art of building meaningful and lasting relationships, it's important to reflect on the core principles that have been woven throughout each chapter. These key concepts—empathy, listening, authenticity, positivity, persuasion, and relationship-building—are the foundation of strong, enduring connections.

Empathy is the gateway to understanding others on a deeper level. When you walk in someone else's shoes, you begin to see the world through their eyes, allowing you to respond thoughtfully to their needs and emotions. The importance of empathy cannot be overstated, as it's the bridge that turns casual interactions into meaningful connections. Listening is another vital piece of this puzzle. In a world where distractions are everywhere, the simple act of truly listening can make all the difference in how others perceive you and how strong your relationships become.

Authenticity, on the other hand, is about embracing who you are and being genuine in your interactions. It is the cornerstone of trust and vulnerability, helping you form connections that are real, not superficial. People are drawn to those who are transparent, open, and comfortable in their own skin. Authenticity means being honest about your feelings and intentions, which fosters deeper, more meaningful connections.

Positivity plays an equally crucial role in creating an environment where others feel uplifted and valued. A positive attitude not only makes you more approachable but also helps you navigate challenges with grace. Positivity is contagious, and it has the power to inspire others, making you a magnet for friends, colleagues, and new opportunities.

Persuasion, when practiced ethically, builds mutual respect and trust. This book has highlighted the difference between influence and manipulation, emphasizing the importance of using persuasion rooted in honesty, integrity, and mutual benefit. By aligning your goals with others and finding common ground, you can create win-win situations where both parties thrive. Healthy persuasion builds relationships based on respect rather than coercion, making your influence lasting and positive.

Relationship-building is a long-term investment, and it requires consistent effort. Friendships and professional connections need to be nurtured over time, not just when it's convenient. Small, meaningful gestures, regular check-ins, and showing appreciation go a long way toward keeping those bonds strong.

Ultimately, sustaining relationships is about balance—between your personal and professional commitments, between giving and receiving, and between independence and connectedness. By practicing these skills and principles consistently, you'll not only maintain your current relationships but also attract new ones.

Every interaction is an opportunity to practice these skills, whether it's through empathy, active listening, or authentic communication. The more you use them, the stronger and more natural they become, allowing you to navigate all areas of life with confidence, kindness, and influence.

Friendships and connections, when nurtured with care, respect, and consistency, become a source of support, inspiration, and fulfillment. As you move forward, remember that building relationships is a continuous journey, one that requires mindfulness and intention but rewards you with lasting influence and genuine bonds.

By refining these principles over time, you'll be well on your way to creating a lifetime filled with meaningful connections, influence, and friendships that stand the test of time.

Applying Lessons in Everyday Life

As you begin to integrate the social strategies discussed throughout this book into your daily interactions, it's essential to approach them with intentionality and consistency. Every relationship, whether personal or professional, offers an opportunity to apply the skills of empathy, listening, authenticity, and positivity. By practicing these behaviors consistently, they will naturally become part of how you engage with the world around you.

Start by making small but significant changes. Focus on truly listening when someone speaks to you—without distractions or interruptions. Practice empathy by considering the perspectives and emotions of others before responding. These subtle shifts can transform your conversations and interactions, creating deeper connections and fostering trust.

Authenticity should remain at the heart of everything you do. Whether you're networking, navigating conflicts, or building influence at work, being true to yourself will strengthen your bonds with others. Stay mindful of being genuine while balancing openness with discretion. People appreciate sincerity, and your willingness to be transparent will draw others toward you.

Positivity and optimism, as explored in previous chapters, are powerful tools for not only attracting people but also for managing challenges. Maintaining a positive attitude in both favorable and difficult situations helps create an environment where others feel valued and motivated. As positivity is contagious, the energy you bring into your interactions can inspire those around you.

Ethical persuasion and influence are also valuable in everyday life. Instead of manipulating or pressuring others, focus on aligning your goals with theirs and finding common ground. By doing so, you can build trust and foster collaborative relationships. This approach strengthens mutual respect and opens doors for personal and professional growth.

It's equally important to cultivate relationships over time by making meaningful gestures, showing appreciation, and being consistent in your interactions. Whether through a thoughtful message, a sincere compliment, or a simple check-in, these efforts help keep relationships alive, even amid busy schedules.

As you apply these lessons, also remember to embrace ongoing personal growth. Relationships are dynamic and constantly evolving, requiring you to adapt and continue learning. Stay open to feedback, reflect on your experiences, and be willing to refine your approach when necessary. The journey to mastering these social strategies is ongoing, but the more you practice, the more natural they will become.

Ultimately, the goal is to enhance your relationships by building genuine connections, fostering trust, and leaving a positive impact on the lives of those around you. With dedication, mindfulness, and a commitment to continuous improvement, these strategies will serve as a solid foundation for personal and professional success.

A Commitment to Lifelong Connection

Building a lifetime of friendship and influence is not a one-time effort but an ongoing process that requires continuous nurturing and dedication. Relationships, whether personal or professional, evolve with time, and so should your approach to maintaining and strengthening them. It's through consistent effort, empathy, and authenticity that you'll foster deeper, more meaningful connections that stand the test of time.

Investing in relationships offers long-term benefits that extend far beyond momentary gains. Personally, cultivating friendships and strong bonds with family creates a network of emotional support, trust, and love. These connections can be a source of comfort, strength, and joy throughout life's various challenges and triumphs. Professionally, building a solid network of meaningful relationships enhances your ability to collaborate, succeed, and grow within your career. Colleagues, mentors, and clients who trust and respect you will be more likely to support your endeavors and offer valuable opportunities in the future.

The real value of building influence through relationships lies in the mutual benefit it creates. Influence, when wielded ethically and with integrity, fosters collaboration, shared success, and lasting respect. It's the people who invest in others, through empathy and genuine connection, who leave a positive and lasting impact on the world around them.

As you continue to practice these skills, they will naturally become a fulfilling part of your life. The small, thoughtful gestures, active listening, and authentic conversations that you engage in daily will shape the foundation of strong, lasting relationships. This journey of connection, built on empathy, authenticity, and mutual respect, will continue to enrich your life both personally and professionally.

Ultimately, the commitment to lifelong connection is about creating a life filled with meaningful relationships, where trust, support, and influence are shared and reciprocated. As you embrace the principles outlined in this book and continue practicing them in your everyday life, you'll find that building and sustaining relationships becomes second nature, bringing greater fulfillment and success to all areas of your life.

How to Make Friends and Influence People: The Modern Guide to Building Lasting Relationships and Personal Influence

Unlock the Power of Connection and Personal Influence

In today's fast-paced, digital world, building authentic, lasting relationships is more important than ever. Whether you're looking to excel in your career, create meaningful friendships, or simply become a more influential person, **"How to Make Friends and Influence People"** offers the tools and strategies you need.

Drawing on timeless principles and modern insights, this guide covers everything from mastering the art of empathy to resolving conflicts, networking like a pro, and sustaining long-term relationships. Each chapter provides actionable advice grounded in emotional intelligence, positivity, and authenticity, making this a practical roadmap to personal growth and influence.

Inside, you'll discover:

- **The Art of Empathy**: How to truly understand others and respond to their needs.
- **Ethical Persuasion Techniques**: Influence people without manipulation by aligning your goals with theirs.
- **The Power of Authenticity**: Build trust and rapport by being genuine and transparent.
- **Resolving Conflicts**: Turn disagreements into opportunities for growth and deeper understanding.
- **Networking Like a Pro**: Expand your social and professional circles with meaningful, lasting connections.
- **Building Influence at Work**: Strengthen your relationships with colleagues and clients, and foster a positive work environment.
- **Sustaining Long-Term Relationships**: Strategies for maintaining friendships and professional connections, even with busy schedules.

With practical tips, real-world examples, and proven strategies, this book will equip you to navigate social interactions with confidence, build stronger relationships, and influence others with integrity. **"How to Make Friends and Influence People"** is your comprehensive guide to becoming the person others respect, admire, and want to connect with—both personally and professionally.

Are you ready to transform the way you connect with the world? Start your journey today!